EMPOWERED!

Claiming the Power of the Holy Spirit

REVISED EDITION

ESTHER BURROUGHS

New Hope® Publishers

Birmingham, Alabama

New Hope® Publishers
P.O. Box 12065
Birmingham, AL 35202-2065
www.newhopepubl.com

© 1999 by New Hope® Publishers
First printing 1999
Printed in the United States

All rights reserved. No part of this publication may be reproduced,
stored in a retrieval system, or transmitted in any form or by any
means—electronic, mechanical, photocopying, recording, or other-
wise—without the prior written permission of the publisher.

Dewey Decimal Classification: 266
Subject Headings: MISSIONS
                                  HOLY SPIRIT
Scripture quotations are from:
King James Version
New King James Version.Copyright © 1982 by Thomas Nelson,
Inc. Used by permission. All rights reserved.
The Living Bible, copyright 1971 by Tyndale House Publishers,
Wheaton, Illinois. Used by permission.
Holy Bible, New International Version. Copyright © 1973, 1978,
1984, International Bible Society.
Used by Permission of Zondervan Bible Publishers.
The Message. Copyright © 1993, 1994, 1995. Used by permission of
NavPress Publishing Group.
NEW AMERICAN STANDARD BIBLE ®,© Copyright The
Lockman Foundation 1960, 1962, 1963, 1968, 1971, 1972, 1973,
1975, 1977. Used by permission.

Cover design by Pat Hooten

ISBN:1-56309-716-8
N994101 • 0899 • 7.5M1

Dedication

I would like the honor
of dedicating this book
to our adult children.
Melody Jean Reid is
our firstborn.
She is my friend . . .
ministry coworker. . .
partner in life's journey . . .
encourager . . .
mother/extraordinaire to our
three precious Grand Girls
and is a Bible study teacher
in her church.
Her choice of a life mate in Will
delights us greatly.
David Lloyd Burroughs
is our second born child.
He is my friend . . .
shares my heartbeat . . .
President of Passport,
Youth Camping with a Mission,
and is the father of our precious Grand
Twins. I admire his gentle ways. His
choice of a life mate in Colleen delights
our hearts.

Contents

1

Fall Fresh on Me

The Holy Spirit—Our Person

Spirit of the Living God, fall fresh on me
Spirit of the Living God, fall fresh on me
Break me, melt me, mold me,
fill me, (use me)
Spirit of the Living God, fall fresh on me.

Daniel Iverson, "Spirit of the Living God"
© 1994 Birdwing. Used by permission.

What a prayer request—that the Holy Spirit
might fall on us like a waterfall: rushing, flowing, constantly moving, cleansing and refreshing all it touches. One of Webster's definitions
of the word *fall* is "to become less, to lose
power." In a very real sense, when you and I
come under the power of the Holy Spirit, we
yield our power—becoming less so that He
can become more. Do you remember the disciples' obedience when Jesus told them to let
down their nets (Luke 5:8)? And do you recall
their reaction when they caught a boatload?
When Simon Peter saw this, he fell at Jesus'
feet. Peter recognized God's power! No
wonder the early church had passion! They
waited for the power to fall fresh on them—
"a fresh wind and fresh fire," as Jim Cymbala

When I fail, it is often because I insist on my way and not on His. I need to be made new and fresh daily through the Holy Spirit's power—on a moment-by-moment basis.

writes in his book by the same title. "But you shall receive power when the Holy Spirit has come upon you; and you shall be witnesses to Me in Jerusalem, and in all Judea and Samaria, and to the end of the earth" (Acts 1:8 NKJV).

Empowered living involves the act of falling down before the highest power, the Holy Spirit. *Fresh*, the dictionary cites, "recently made, new, and bold." The idea is that something is so recent that it has fresh- ness—which is exactly how you feel when the Spirit has taught you something, or when He has shown Himself clearly to you. To be empowered by the Holy Spirit—in the process of being continually remade—is over- whelmingly exciting to me. When I fail, it is often because I insist on my way and not on His. I need to be made new and fresh daily through the Holy Spirit's power—on a moment-by-moment basis. We can live in the knowledge that the fresh wind and fire of the Holy Spirit are working through us even when we don't feel it or least expect it. This is not only amazing—it is true!

The word *empower* means "to give power to, to authorize, to enable." *To enable* means to provide with power. This definition affirms Paul's assurance to the Ephesians that the Holy Spirit empowers and enables us "according to the power that works in us" (Eph. 3:20 NKJV). I have chosen this verse, Ephesians 3:20, as the theme for this book. Many are the times God has used this verse in my own life's journey. Look with me at the larger pas- sage in which verse 20 is found:

*For this reason, I bow my knees to the
Father of our Lord Jesus Christ, from whom
the whole family in heaven and earth is named,
that He would grant you, according to the
riches of His glory, to be strengthened with
might through His Spirit in the inner man;
that Christ may dwell in your hearts through
faith; and that you, being rooted and grounded
in love, may be able to comprehend with all the
saints what is the width and length and depth
and height—to know the love of Christ which
passes knowledge; that you may be filled with
all the fullness of God. Now to Him who is
able to do exceedingly abundantly above all
that we ask or think, according to the power
that works within us, to Him be the glory in
the church by Christ Jesus to all generations
forever and ever. Amen (Eph. 3:14–21
NKJV).*

The Holy Spirit Is a Person

Where did we get the notion that the Holy
Spirit is an "it"? The Holy Spirit is a person.
Jesus, the Son of God, came in the flesh and
lived out His life as a physical being, moving
about in physical space and doing the will of
God. Jesus completed His work on the cross.
He even spoke from the cross the words, "It is
finished." He accomplished what God sent
Him to do. The Lord Jesus came, suffered,
died, rose again, and went back to heaven to
sit at the right hand of God, His Father. Why
did He sit down? His work on earth was

finished. He waited forty days and then He sent the Holy Spirit to take up His work on earth. Since Jesus' redeeming work on the cross, God has chosen to work through the person and power of the Holy Spirit.

Have you ever felt the urge to pray for someone, but then just said, "I'll pray for him later"? Or has anyone ever called you and said, "I need you to pray for me; I have this need…"? A missionary on furlough told this true story while visiting his home church in Michigan:

While serving at a small field hospital in Africa, every two weeks I traveled by bicycle through the jungle to a nearby city for supplies. This was a journey of two days and required camping overnight at the halfway point. On one of these journeys I arrived in the city where I planned to collect money from a bank and get supplies. Then I would begin my two-day journey back to the field hospital. Upon arriving in the city I observed two men fighting, one of whom had been seriously injured. I treated him for his injuries and at the same time talked to him about the Lord Jesus Christ. I then traveled two days, camping overnight, and arrived home without incident. Two weeks later I repeated my journey. Upon arriving in the city, I was approached by the young man I had treated. He told me that he had known I carried money and medicines.

He said, "Some friends and I followed you into the jungle, knowing you would camp overnight. *We planned to kill you and take your money and drugs. But just as we were about to move into your camp we saw that you were surrounded by twenty-six armed guards."*

At this I laughed, and said that I was certainly all alone out in that jungle campsite. The young man pressed the point, however, and said, *"No sir! I was not the only person to see the guards. My five friends also saw them, and we all counted them. It was because of those guards that we were afraid and left you alone."* At this point in the testimony, one of the men in the congregation stood to his feet and interrupted the missionary, asking if he could tell him the exact day that this happened.

The missionary told him the date, and the man who had interrupted told him this story:

"On the night of your incident in Africa, it was morning here and I was preparing to go play golf. I was about to putt when I felt the urge to pray for you. In fact, the urging of the Lord was so strong that I called men in this church to meet with me in the sanctuary to pray for you."

Then he said, *"Would all of those men who met with me on that day stand up?"*

The men who had met together to pray that day stood up. The missionary wasn't concerned with who they were—he was too busy counting how many men he saw. There were twenty-six!

The Holy Spirit dwells in us. As Jesus was with the disciples, so the Holy Spirit is within us. He is as close to us as our very breath.

When we commit ourselves to the Lord, all that we do is fueled by the enabling power and presence of the Holy Spirit.

This story is an incredible example of how the Spirit of the Lord moves in mysterious ways. Nothing is ever hurt by prayer except the gates of hell.

The person of the Holy Spirit manages the circumstances of our lives, bringing glory to God. We should know the Holy Spirit as intimately as the disciples knew Jesus. They walked, talked, prayed, and ate with Jesus. We can do the same! The Holy Spirit dwells in us. As Jesus was with the disciples, so the Holy Spirit is within us. He is as close to us as our very breath. In fact, we should pray "let Your Spirit loose," rather than "let your Holy Spirit fall"!

The Holy Spirit Is the Sent One

We did not ask for the Holy Spirit. Jesus sent Him, saying not only that He, the Holy Spirit, would comfort us, but that He would help us do greater works than Jesus did!

Listen to what Jesus said about the Holy Spirit:

But now, I am going to Him who sent Me; but I tell you the truth, it is to your advantage that I go away; for if I do not go away, the Helper shall not come to you, but if I go, I will send Him to you   (John 6:5–15).

God sent the Holy Spirit—a member of the Godhead—to walk among us without any limitations of time and space. It is through the ministry of the Holy Spirit that every other ministry God has provided and His Son has purchased becomes real to us. He is the God inside us. He is the God who makes all things real to us.

Remember: The Holy Spirit is the Sent One. We did not ask for Him. In that Jesus was God-man, He was bound by His physical extremities— limited by His physical body. The person of the Holy Spirit has no limitations. He does not have a physical body. He reveals Himself to us in many different ways.

The Sent One, this Holy Spirit, is omnipresent. This means not so much that He is everywhere present, as it means that He is in one place and in one heart as if He were in no other. This is a powerful thought. He has worked and still works specifically in my life.

Think about it this way: In any given Sunday worship service or retreat, as the speaker delivers the message, a woman on the left side of the room has tears streaming down her face, indicating that the Spirit is at work in her heart. At the same time, someone on the right side of the room is having an experience with the Spirit. And in the middle of the same audience someone may be jotting down a grocery list!

The Spirit is everywhere present and, thankfully, specifically present in each of our hearts, working to bring glory to God.

Think of it: The Holy Spirit dwells right within you and me. The Holy Spirit of God calls us to be the temple of God, and He dwells in us. This is a profound thought when we consider what it encompasses. When we commit ourselves to the Lord, all that we do is fueled by the enabling power and presence of the Holy Spirit.

The Holy Spirit is God's seal on our lives, His promise that we now belong to Him. The Spirit says, "This soul belongs to Me. I dwell here now, and I will never leave!"

Also, consider this: We do not need to cry for the Heavenly Dove to come among us. The Holy Spirit is here, not because we plead for Him to come, but because He was sent by Jesus! Jesus Christ came into the world for a specific purpose: to do the work of the cross. The Holy Spirit has come into the world for a specific purpose as well: to do God's work in and through the life of every believer.

The Deity of this Sent One is revealed in the names given Him:
- Spirit of the Son of God
  - Eternal Spirit
    - Holy Spirit
      - Holy Ghost

When we talk about this Sent One, we are talking about Holy God. The Spirit is a living, powerful witness of God, sent to change all humankind. He has power to love, so He has emotion. He has power to know all things, so He has knowledge. He has volition, so He has the power to will. This Sent One has come to live within you and me so that we can do whatever God has called us to do!

The Holy Spirit Is the Saving One

The work of the Holy Spirit is to draw us to Christ. When we ask Jesus Christ to enter our hearts, we are responding to the call of the Holy Spirit.

Notice how the Father, the Son, and the Spirit work together. God, the Father, has sent the Son. The Son has sent the Holy Spirit. The Holy Spirit is now working to secure us a place in the family of God. The Holy Spirit, the Sent One, is the witness at our adoption into the family of God. We often don't emphasize this important truth with new Christians. We seem to hesitate to tell them the whole story. We are not alone when we begin our journey as new believers! In days of old, when the king sent a message, it was sealed in wax with his signature. The recipient knew immediately who had sent the message. The Holy Spirit is God's seal on our lives, His promise that we now belong to Him. The Spirit says, "This soul belongs to Me. I dwell here now, and I will never leave!"

The Holy Spirit Is our Adoption Agent

Paul wrote to the Romans,

For all who are being led by the Spirit of God, these are the sons of God. For you have not received a spirit of slavery leading to fear again, but you received the Spirit of adoption as sons by which we cry out, "Abba, Father." The Spirit Himself bears witness with our spirit that we are children of God, and if children, heirs also, heirs of God and fellow heirs with Christ, if indeed we suffer with Him, that we may be glorified with Him (Rom. 8:14–17 NASV).

We have been adopted as sons and daughters. Not only does the Spirit adopt, He seals the adoption (Gal. 4:5). "In Him, you also, after listening to the message of truth, the gospel of your salvation—having also believed, you were sealed in Him with the Holy Spirit of promise, who is given as a pledge of our inheritance, with a view to the redemption of God's own possession to the praise of His glory" (Eph. 1:13-14 NASV).

The Holy Spirit is the "whisper of God's love." He possesses all of God's attributes. He is fully God. Throughout history God has disclosed His personal presence through the Holy Spirit. In Old Testament stories the Holy Spirit was given to an individual at a specific time to aid in accomplishing a particular assignment. From the beginning of time we see the triune of God at work. Colossians 1:13-17 verifies the work of the Triune God, showing Christ's intricate involvement in creation.

The Spirit does what only God can do. Since Jesus was conceived of the Holy Spirit and since Jesus is the Son of God, the Spirit is God. In John 6:38, we see that Jesus the Son never does anything on His own, He does only what He sees the Father doing.

In Genesis 1:26 God says, "Let us (that would be God the Father, Son and Holy Spirit) make man in our image." Beth Moore, in her study, *Breaking Free,* says of Deuteronomy 6:4 (NIV) that on Lord accomplished all of creation through the Father's will, the Son's Word, and the Spirit's way. This same Holy Spirit who hovered over creation, speaks of Himself as the "Word" in John 1:1. *The Message* translation says, "and the Word became flesh and moved into the neighborhood. The third *person* of the three in one God, is the energizing power of the Godhead. Remember you and I live in the empowering of the Holy Spirit, because of

the gift of God the Father in sending God the
Son, and the gift of the Son in sending the
Holy Spirit. Do not separate the work of the
three. Three in one, One in three.

Throughout history, God has disclosed His
personal presence through the Holy Spirit. In
the Old Testament, the Holy Spirit is sometimes seen working through an individual at a
specific time to aid in accomplishing a particular assignment.

However, with the coming of the Holy
Spirit in the New Testament until the end of
time, the Holy Spirit works in the same way,
though He indwells each believer. Through
the filling of the Holy Spirit believers are
equipped for service (Eph. 5:18–31; Rom. 12).

We know the person of the Holy Spirit
as a person because He has called us into a
personal relationship with Jesus. The Spirit's
power, through God's love, touched our
hearts, inviting us to accept Christ. The
minute we accepted Christ as Savior and
Lord, the Holy Spirit came to dwell in our
inner being.

"Having believed, you were sealed with the
Holy Spirit of promise, who is the guarantee
of our inheritance until the redemption of the
purchased possession, to the praise of His
glory" (Eph. 1:13, 14 NKJV).

This experience of salvation is called the
"baptism of the Holy Spirit." The filling of
the Holy Spirit is a continual process. We will
talk about this later in Chapter Four. But
mark it down: It was the person of the Holy
Spirit that whispered, nudged, or impressed
you and me, drawing us to Jesus.

The Holy Spirit Is the Teacher/Guide

"God is Spirit, and those who worship Him must worship in spirit and in truth."
—John 4:24

"If you abide in My word, you are My disciples indeed. And you shall know the truth, and the truth shall make you free."
—John 8:31, 32

Remember: Truth is a person.

When the Helper comes, whom I shall send to you from the Father, that is the Spirit of truth, who proceeds from the Father, He will bear witness of Me" (John 15:26 NASV).

"However, when He, the Spirit of truth, has come, He will guide you into all truth; for He will not speak on His own authority, but whatever He hears He will speak; and He will tell you things to come (John 16:13).

Think of this when you read the Word of God and are drawn to a certain verse as if it was just the word of encouragement, correction, or guidance you need. The Holy Spirit is speaking to you. When you are listening to a Bible teacher or your pastor, and the words cut right to your heart, the Holy Spirit is speaking to you. My friend Henry Blackaby says, "When I am teaching, you hear more than I say. That is the Holy Spirit teaching you as I teach . . . ." He is speaking of the loving whisper of the teaching Holy Spirit.

The Holy Spirit Is the Helper

In her book *Step Into the Water*, Peg Rankin writes:

Jesus tells the disciples who the Spirit is. Jesus speaks. Is He going to introduce His own Spirit? You wonder. Why, that must be like introducing Himself. You listen intently. I want to acquaint you with the Spirit of the Sovereign Lord, Jesus begins. The One who is upon Me, the One who has anointed Me to preach the good news to the poor, to bind up the broken-hearted, to proclaim freedom for the captives and release from darkness or the prisoners, He is the Spirit of Truth. He goes out from the Father. He testifies about Me. And He brings glory to Me. He descended upon Me at My water baptism in the form of a dove. But He will baptize you with fire. He led Me to the place of temptation and then enabled Me to stand firm against the onslaughts of Satan. He will do the same for you. When I told my disciples I would send 'another Helper,' Jesus continues, I was referring to Someone like Myself, yet different. Whereas I was the first helper, He is the second. I dwelt among My people. He dwells within them. I was a temporary resident of Earth; He is a more permanent One. I came in physical form; He, spiritual. Those who receive Me receive My Spirit, who then becomes 'a spring of water, welling up to eternal life.'

Dear sisters in Christ, we can live in the power of the Spring of Living Water that flows through our lives and touches our world. This Holy Spirit invites us to step into the river of life and let Him direct and carry us as we place our trust in Him.

Dear sisters in Christ, we can live in the power of the Spring of Living Water that flows through our lives and touches our world. This Holy Spirit invites us to step into the river of life and let Him direct and carry us as we place our trust in Him.

The Holy Spirit Is the Third Person of the Trinity

The triune God is three persons-in-one and one person-in-three. This is a faith issue! I do not understand how water can be liquid, ice, and steam. I do know when I need each of these elements. Another way to look at the three-in-one concept is this: A man and a woman—one in marriage—have three roles: son/daughter, father/mother, grandfather/grandmother. In fact, each role carries a different name! Between Bob and me, we have four roles: Bob/Esther, husband/wife, dad/mom, Bop/Nana—all referring to the same individuals! The same person, the Holy Spirit, carries out different role responsibilities. God the Father sent Jesus the Son. Jesus the Son sent the Holy Spirit.

Once, while teaching about the Holy Spirit at a meeting out West, I heard a voice in the audience say "Preach it, Sister!" I looked around to find its source, only to hear my husband—who was also on the platform—say, "She means you, honey!" Encouraged, I went on to say, "If you only trust the work of God the Father and God the Son, you only have two-thirds of the power." At this my sister-in-Christ responded, "Oh, no, honey! You ain't got no power!" I stand corrected. The power indeed rests in the presence of the Holy Spirit.

The Holy Spirit Is our Comforter and our Cover

The name Comforter describes one attribute of the Holy Spirit. A comforter is a quilted cover that gives comfort. The Holy Spirit covers and comforts us like a quilt. My daughter, Melody, loved Fluffy, a pink satin comforter given to Bob and me as a wedding gift. It comforted Melody, and made it through two of her three daughters before it disintegrated. Many times when life brought pain, that comforter wrapped Melody in security and comfort. The Holy Spirit is our cover forever. And He never wears out!

Several years ago I was captivated by a passage in Judges 6. It says here that the Spirit of the Lord came upon Gideon—the phrase "came upon" literally means clothed. When the angel of the Lord appeared to Gideon on the threshing floor, Gideon was absolutely terrified and awed, as he had great respect for the holiness of God. Literally rendered, the text says that the Spirit of Yahweh "dressed Himself" with Gideon. The human agent became the outer appearance through which the Spirit worked.

As I read this, my heart was stirred. I prayed, "O God, clothe me with Your Spirit!" I then envisioned God's Spirit clothing me.

Now with each new day, I breathe this prayer: "Oh God, clothe me today with Your Spirit." What an awesome concept! I am clothed with God. I like the idea of God

Just imagine what He could do with you and me if we would cooperate with what the Holy Spirit wants to do through us.

clothing me and wrapping Himself around me. Indeed, He does just that!

There is another perspective in this image. God clothed Himself with Gideon and set about doing His work through Gideon. God dressed Himself with Gideon that day in order to do His work. Just imagine what He could do with you and me if we would cooperate with what the Holy Spirit wants to do through us. The Spirit of God disguised Himself in Gideon. What a surprise for the Midianite Army!

So God and I are clothed in and with each other—living daily in each other. I walk into my world clothed (dressed) with the Spirit of God, and God walks into my world clothed (dressed) with me. Isn't this incredible? Consider what God can do in your life through the Holy Spirit because He has clothed Himself with you. You can be empowered by His Holy Spirit.

This same idea is found in Romans 13:14: "Clothe yourselves with the Lord Jesus Christ, and do not think about how to gratify the desires of the sinful nature" (NIV). Paul exhorts us to dress or clothe ourselves in a Spiritual nature. To put on the Spiritual nature is to put on a new garment—Jesus Himself.Clothed with Jesus, we live according to His guidance rather than follow the old nature of the flesh. Paul reminds us that we are to put on "the whole armor of God. We are to clothe ourselves with the breastplate of righteousness, the shield of faith, the helmet of salvation, and the Sword of the Spirit, which is the Word of God" (Eph. 6:10–18).

The Old Testament reference to being "clothed by God" fits beautifully with the New Testament reference. Paul uses the metaphor of a soldier who possesses only one offensive weapon: the Word of God. Isaiah wrote:

I will greatly rejoice in the lord, My soul shall be joyful in my God; for He has clothed me with the garments of salvation, He has covered me with the robe of righteousness, As a bridegroom decks himself with ornaments, And as a bride adorns herself with jewels. For as the earth brings its bud, As the garden causes the things that are sown in it to spring forth, So the Lord God will cause righteousness and praise to spring forth before all nations (Isa. 61:10–11 NKJV).

What a precious thought—that God would call us to Himself through His Son, Jesus, giving us the garment of salvation and clothing us in the garment of His righteousness. He clothes us and covers us in the perfect righteousness of God.

We sing, "dressed in His righteousness alone, faultless to stand before the throne." Then He promises to clothe us in the power of His Holy Spirit. I want to dress like that, don't you?

"Now when they saw the boldness of Peter and John, and perceived that they were uneducated and untrained men, they marveled. And they realized they had been with Jesus" (Acts 4:13).

Concerning this passage, Oswald Chambers writes, "Complete abandon to the love of Christ is the one thing that bears fruit in the life, and it will always leave the impression of the holiness and of the power of God—never our personal holiness." It is not a prideful thing when we see the Holy Spirit work. We are humbled when we recognize that the Holy Spirit works through us as His vessels.

Many years ago my precious father taught me this important lesson: "Before you speak publicly, Esther, always give the message back to God. Lay it down before Him. Give it to Him in prayer. Then it is His message and not yours." I follow his advice every time I speak, asking God to work through me, His vessel.

While attending an Aspiring Women's Conference, I was stopped by a young woman whose church had hosted the conference.

She said, "I was a college student, and was at a conference in New Mexico when I heard you speak the closing night. I came to the altar that night under God's call on my life. I'll never forget what you shared about splashing the Living Water. My husband is on the staff of this church, and I am leading in the women's ministry team with women in this church. We call our ministry 'Sharing the Living Water'. Thank you for your influence in my life."

Holy! Holy! Holy! We never know how the Spirit will use us to bear fruit for His Kingdom. I often ponder what might happen in the evangelical world if Christians were immediately obedient to the whisper of the Holy Spirit. We live in a world immersed

with noise. Have you ever said in frustration,
"It's so noisy that I can't hear myself think!"
My suspicion is that we seldom get quiet
enough to hear the still small voice of God—
the whisper of the Holy Spirit.

In his delightful and powerful book, *My
Utmost for His Highest*, Oswald Chambers
writes, "The voice of the Spirit is as gentle as
a zephyr, so gentle that unless you are living
in perfect communion with God, you never
hear it." The Holy Spirit often comes as a
still, small voice—so small that unless we are
listening we will never notice it.

In this noise-infested world where we live,
we are rarely quiet enough to hear the Spirit
of God. In our busy, fast-paced lives, unless
we take time daily to listen for the Holy
Spirit's voice, we will never know what the
Holy Spirit is able to do in and for us. We
find it easy to say that only the "special saints"
know what it is like to have the Spirit of God
in their lives. This is not true! God has
clothed each of us as He did Gideon, and He
will work through our lives, too, if we give
Him opportunity.

- Be still enough to hear the Spirit's
  whisper.
- Busyness is the greatest deterrent to
  the Spirit's work today.
- Embrace the presence of the Spirit
  every day—in every way.
- Release the Spirit's power through
  faith and obedience.

2

Break Me

The Holy Spirit—Our Purifier

Consume me with a fire
that will purify my soul.

David Clydesdale, "Purify Me, Lord" © Word Entertainment

When my church choir sings this chorus,
I weep silently. I know that there are private
corners that I withhold from the Holy Spirit.
I long for the warmth and peace of the Holy
Spirit's presence. I long for the Spirit to purify
my soul. I am always glad when we sing this
hymn, as it sings itself into my heart for days
and gently reminds me of the convicting
power of the Holy Spirit.

To break means to disclose, to penetrate, to
interrupt—an interruption of regularity.

Look at Jesus' relationship with the Holy
Spirit. Jesus knows Him best. Jesus lived intimately and walked daily with the Holy Spirit.
All that Jesus taught us was out of His harmo-
nious fellowship with the Spirit. Jesus desires
that you and I live in holy intimacy with the
Holy Spirit. Think of this: At every important
event in Jesus' life, the Holy Spirit was present. The Holy Spirit came upon the Virgin
Mary at Jesus' conception. The Holy Spirit

came as a dove at His baptism. The Holy
Spirit was present when Jesus was tempted.
The Holy Spirit labored with Jesus through-
out His earthly ministry. In the New
Testament, you will not find even one refer-
ence to the Holy Spirit associating with any
one individual until after Jesus' resurrection!
I am amazed by this observation. The Holy
Spirit focused His energy on Jesus as He made
His way to the cross. What an enabling
message for you and me: This same Holy
Spirit is available to work in each of us, just
as He worked in Jesus.

In Matthew we read, "The virgin will be
with child and will give birth to a son, and
they will call him 'Immanuel'—which means,
'God with us' " (Matt. 1:23 NIV). Matthew
begins his Gospel with this announcement:
that God will be with us. He closes his Gospel
with Jesus' announcement that all authority in
heaven and on earth has been given to Him,
and the commission that we are to make disciples of all nations. The book ends with the
same promise: "Lo, I am with you always,
even to the end of the age" (Matt. 28:20
NASV).

Jesus, true to His word, promised the disciples that they would be filled with the Holy
Spirit. He told them that He was going to
leave someone with them who would do
greater things in them than He was able to
do—the Holy Spirit. The person of the Holy
Spirit is within each of us, refining us for
service, never leaving us alone in the process.
We are living in the day of the Holy Spirit. In
Old Testament days the work was done by

The Holy Spirit focused His energy on Jesus as He made His way to the cross.

God, the Father, through many prominent people. Then Jesus came. In the New Testament Jesus was the prominent one— doing the work and carrying out the plans of God. Since the resurrection, God's work is accomplished through the empowerment of His Holy Spirit in willing and obedient Christians. We have only to ask the Holy Spirit continually to do the things in us that the Scripture says are His ministry.

The Ministry of the Holy Spirit:
Conviction and Control

Only by yielding to the Holy Spirit's purifying and controlling power will we have the victory we desire. Jesus said it was good for Him to go away—that this would be best for us. "The Son is the radiance of God's glory and the exact representation of His being, sustaining all things by his powerful word" (Heb. 1:3 NIV).

Jesus finished His work as our Savior. Then He sat down at the right hand of God and sent the Holy Spirit. Paul exhorted the Ephesians, "Be filled with the Spirit" (Eph. 5:18 NKJV). By this he meant that being filled is a continual process. To receive the Holy Spirit into our lives is not so much like putting gas in our car; it is more like putting the Holy Spirit in the driver's seat. Through the controlling power of the Holy Spirit, we maintain our relationship with God and give Him ownership of our lives. As the Spirit has His way in us, He produces fruit: " . . . love, joy, peace, longsuffering, kindness, goodness, faithfulness, gentleness, and self-control . . . If we live in the Spirit, let us also walk in the Spirit" (Gal. 5:22–25 NKJV). When the Holy Spirit is in the driver's seat, God is in complete control. When I am in the driver's seat, guess who's in control? I must move out of the driver's seat so He can move in. Consider this: Your doing may have become a substitute for His doing.

When circumstances of life—stress, family, relationships, or sin—cause me to need an attitude adjustment, the Spirit can take over, enabling me to confess, move out of the driver's seat, and let Him have the wheel. Think of it this way: The Holy Spirit moves between a convicting and controlling ministry. He is either controlling us or convicting us.

Sometimes, as the Spirit convicts us, we become aware that the fruits of the Spirit are no longer a vital part of our lives. Love, joy, peace, and all the rest have "flown the coop." We have all been there. Each of us could tell our story. "This 'control stuff' happens to me over and over," you say. "What can I do about it?" It's quite simple, really. Ask the Spirit to cleanse you and fill you. Then yield to Him. Confess the sin; ask the Spirit to fill you. Then make way for Him to move out of that convicting seat and into the controlling seat! To "be filled" is not a passive act. It is an active and continuous act of depending on God. To be filled with the Spirit means that we:

- Take our hands off the wheel,
- Ask the Holy Spirit to be the driver,
- Trust Him to do His work,
- Actively listen for His voice, then
- Celebrate His power.

Relinquishing Control to the Holy Spirit

The winter of 1989 brought a permanent change to my life. Our son, David, was serving in Vail, Colorado, as a semester missionary. My husband, Bob, and I had accepted an engagement to speak at a seminary in California, so we planned to stop by Vail to visit David for a few days.

David urged me several times, "Mom, you really should try skiing! The powder here is great!" (I'd thought powder was something you put on your face.) "This is the place to ski!" I told David I was too old to learn to ski. He insisted: "You're not old, Mom!" That did it—I was hooked.

After arriving in Vail and getting settled in at our hotel, we went to the ski mountain. Everyone looked great in ski outfits. I decided that skiing might be worth the effort—just to wear those great clothes! It was snowing, and I guess there was a part of me that really wanted to ski. David kept saying, "Mom, you can do it!" So I gave in and tried.

After two wonderful hours on the "bunny slope," we moved up one level. As fate would have it, I fell after getting off the ski lift, and broke my right arm—a clean break! The Ski Patrol came, checked me out, then skied me down the slopes to the hospital. After the doctor looked at my arm, he pronounced those dreaded words: "You are out of business for a few months."

As I boarded the plane to fly back to Atlanta, I began to learn a completely different lifestyle. There was very little I could do

for myself—my right arm was placed at my
waist in an elastic velcro wrap. I was totally
dependent upon someone else, even for the
simplest things—things I had taken for
granted. My husband normally does the
cooking in our house, while my job is cleaning up. But for six weeks he prepared the
meals, cut up my food, fed me, and cleaned
up. My husband had to dress me, bathe me,
and try to do my hair. (You should have seen
my first hairdo when he finished!)

Travel had made me a rather independent
person, and I was accustomed to taking care
of myself. As you might imagine, it was very
difficult for me to need someone else to care
for my every need. And the most disgusting
thing about the whole event was that Bob
took care of me in such a gentle, kind way.
Bob has the gift of mercy—which I'm sure I
do not have! (I've taken a "spiritual gifts test"
several times, *trying* to get the gift of mercy,
but I always fail.)

I kept thinking that if just once he would
act upset, angry, tired, or discouraged, I would
have found the experience a bit easier to
endure. Early each morning Bob would light
a fire in the fireplace. After coffee and devo-
tions he would go down to his office and
leave me with my Bible, devotional books,
and fresh coffee.

I would then sit before the fire, which
brought warmth and healing to my soul. I
cherished this time I spent with the Father,
His Love Letter (the Bible) open before me. I
did several things during this time of inactiv-
ity: I walked through the Bible and found all

of the promises God had given to me through my life's journey, finding when and where He had given them. He showed me all of the places He had taken me as we walked together. When I would glance at the clock, it would already be noon—how quickly the hours had passed!

A stillness began to enter my life. I began to sort out where I had been in the driver's seat, and where I needed to let the Holy Spirit take over. During this period when I could do absolutely nothing for myself, I realized anew that the Holy Spirit wants me to be as totally dependent on Him just as I was now dependent upon my husband. When the Holy Spirit gives us the promises, "Immanuel, God is with us!" and "Lo, I am with you always," He intends for us to trust Him!

Learning to use my arm again was a long and painful experience. One day, just about the time I thought I could stand it no longer, Bob sent me to the family room to take a nap. While I rested he fixed a candlelight dinner. I was overwhelmed again by Bob's kindness, care, and love. I wasn't very romantic, crying through the meal as he fed and cared for me. But I learned a beautiful truth about the Holy Spirit that evening. Bob was not trying to teach me something—he was just being himself. The Holy Spirit is waiting for a chance just to be Himself through us as well.

John Westerhoff, an Episcopal priest, was invited to speak to a youth camp. By the second afternoon, everyone was in a stir because many wallets and purses had been emptied. Rumors began to fly about who had

seen whom in which rooms. That evening the
leader gathered the group together, saying,
"We won't leave this room until the person
who stole the money confesses." You can
imagine the looks that began to fly and the
whispers that traveled across the room.
Standing at the back and observing this, John
was moved to intervene. He quietly made his
way to the front and said to the teens, "We
have come to worship and celebrate this
week. Many here have been wronged, and
you feel angry and frustrated. Let's pray, asking
the Spirit to show us what to do." John then
prayed, "Father, I ask for healing in this group
of teenagers. We trust you, Holy Spirit, to
gently speak conviction to the one who has
wronged us, and we pray that you will remind
each of us of his or her own sin. Help us to
be forgiving and accepting." Before John
could add the "Amen" to the prayer, he felt
the tug of a small boy at his shirt sleeve.

The boy motioned for John to bend
down. He then whispered in John's ear, "I did
it, Sir, and I'm sorry. I will give it all back."
Smiling towards the group, John announced
the confession.

At that point the leader jumped up in
front of the group and took control of the
situation and grabbed the boy. He began to
chide him for stealing and gruffly announced
that he was to give the money back and then
he was to be sent back home immediately. A
hush fell over the room...no one breathed,
when from the back row, a voice boomed out,
"Let him stay!" Quickly word spread across
the room like breath from heaven, as the

chant grew louder and louder, "Let him stay!
Let him stay! Let him stay!" The leader,
caught off guard for a second, grasped the
truth and hugged the boy as he joined the
message of redemption, "Let him stay!"

In the quiet spirit of prayer, releasing the
convicting power of the Spirit, confession was
made and grace was given. It was the powerful work of the convicting and controlling
Spirit. It must have felt like the purifying
work of Pentecost! Luke 11:20 reminds us
that the Spirit is pointing God's finger that
sent the demons on their way. God is the
head, Jesus the arm of salvation, and God's
work is carried out, through the Holy Spirit,
the finger of God.

As I began to build back my arm muscles
painfully stretching them—almost more
painful than the accident itself—I began to
improve little by little. I laugh now when I
think how my Bob made progress marks on
the shower and would encourage me to move
to the next line promising an ice cream cone
if I succeeded!

The Holy Spirit also calls us to Himself.
"Trust me, Esther." "Listen to me, Esther."
"Move out of the driver's seat, Esther."
"Exercise your spiritual discipline, Esther."

My progress was based on my discipline to
do the exercises faithfully and regularly. With
exercise, I regained full control and use of my
arm. As I got to the place where I could do
most things for myself, I let go of the discipline of my exercise program. Isn't that just
like us? God's power begins to work in our
lives, we see what He does, and the next

thing we do is strike out on our own. Looking back, I know that I was going through a purifying process. To purify is to cleanse and make pure. The very fact that I thought I could do everything by myself was a deep indication of how deeply I needed to understand the purifying work of the Holy Spirit.

It's a cultural thing to be "driven"—not just when we are driving our car, but driving our lives. You in the driver's seat and the Holy Spirit as a passenger, when it should be the opposite. Being driven is about proving oneself. The plain truth is it is about pride and pride is sin. The sin of pride is almost always about self. Take courage out there in the family of God!

During the six week period of healing from the ski accident, I wrote in my Bible with my left hand and it looks very ragged, just like my life at the time, so I am constantly reminded of the purifying time in my life before the fire. Today, I love it in my quiet time when I happen across one of the verses that the Holy Spirit showed me as He purified my life. My handwriting is unclear. It is a constant reminder of what my life looks like to the Father when I am in control, producing out-of-control living. The lines of authority are blurred. The lifestyle is unintelligible. The life is not abandoned to the Father.

The Spirit's presence in us is the promise of Jesus to us. Our response should be to continue daily, hourly to surrender our lives to Him and allow the Holy Spirit to work through us. As we trust Him, He works. The

If we choose to live in the power of the Holy Spirit, we discover hope in place of despair, courage in place of fear, power in place of weakness, love in place of hate, and faith in every circumstance.

Holy Spirit does not wish to have our plans, but our lives so that He has us and may then work His plan in us. It is one thing to work for God; it is quite another thing to realize that God works through us.

Did you ever hear someone say, "She is so full of the Spirit of God," as if the person speaking was not? Remember that the Holy Spirit in you is God's seal or promise that you are His. In Ephesians 5:18 (TLB), the instructions for us are to . . . be filled with the Holy Spirit. Filling us with the Holy Spirit is God's way of nurturing, growing, and equipping us for service. The sad part is that so many of us accept Jesus Christ as Savior, but we never allow the Holy Spirit to help us grow. We never move to the point of yielding or surrendering our lives to Him so that we can continue to grow and be equipped as saints to do the work of Christ in our world.

Sometimes it frightens us to think about the Spirit's controlling power. It means we live under His convicting power—to yield and surrender. When we yield to someone, we give way, we move back, we stand aside, or we simply get out of the way. That's what a yielding means. My husband doesn't understand this, for as we drive, he thinks yield means a quick look and then an opportunity to go first, then you follow. This is a beautiful word picture of what the Holy Spirit does through us! Once we receive the Holy Spirit, if we do not move aside and yield to Him, then we live without His power. It is no wonder Christians often feel powerless! Christians who do not yield to the Holy

Spirit within them are disobedient. I find it ironic that when we get into trouble we cry out to God for help, as if the Holy Spirit were not within us—already at work. Instead of crying out, perhaps we should cry within. This is where the Spirit of God is—within us.

One New Testament image attributed to the Holy Spirit is "wind." John wrote, "The wind blows wherever it pleases. You hear its sound, but you cannot tell where it comes from or where it is going. So it is with everyone born of the Spirit" (John 3:8 NIV). In this verse we learn that the Spirit has freedom and mystery.

The Greek word for the Spirit is *pneuma.* Like the wind, the Spirit is at liberty to move about exactly as He pleases. He works to renew us and draw us to God. Also like the wind, the movement of the Holy Spirit is mysterious. We cannot see the wind but we can see the effects of its movement—bending limbs, a drifting leaf, or homes destroyed by strong winds. Likewise, we cannot see the Spirit. We can only see the effects of His work, such as the changed life of a person who has been born again. This freedom and mystery of the Spirit reflects His divinity: Only God is utterly free and utterly mysterious. Perhaps this is why we struggle to understand the Holy Spirit. We want to be in control; we are not willing to trust the wind of the Spirit.

We cannot see the wind but we can see the effects of its movement—bending limbs, a drifting leaf, or homes destroyed by strong winds. Likewise, we cannot see the Spirit. We can only see the effects of His work, such as the changed life of a person who has been born again.

Joy in Surrender:
The Controlling Work of the Spirit
Paul writes that in Christ's presence is the

fullness of God, and prays that we may "know the love of Christ which surpasses knowledge, that [we] may be filled up to all of the fullness of God" (Eph. 3:19 NASV).

God wants this to happen in our lives, and the only way it's going to happen is through the power of the Holy Spirit. So, what is the secret of the Holy Spirit's coming in? Every child of God has received the gift of the Holy Spirit. The secret is to *yield* and *surrender*. If my life isn't abundant in Him, it is not because He has not come in, but because I have not surrendered to Him. One of the marks of the Holy Spirit in a believer's life is joy.

Jesus said, "Abide in me and I in you" (John 15:4 NKJV). *To abide* means to stay, to remain in a place where you already are. As believers, we are the sanctuary, the holy place, where the Spirit abides.

When Stephen was stoned, he looked to Jesus—not to his circumstances. As he was being stoned, he was lifted into the presence of the Holy Spirit. By himself he could never have said, "Lord, do not hold this sin against them" (Acts 7:60 NIV). But through the power of the Holy Spirit, God enabled him to do this. When we are empowered by the Holy Spirit, He abides in us and we abide in Him.

We have a choice: We can live in our own power, or we can live in the power of the Holy Spirit. If we choose to live in the power of the Holy Spirit, we discover hope in place of despair, courage in place of fear, power in place of weakness, love in place of hate, and faith in every circumstance. With the Psalmist let us declare, "Every morning I lay out the pieces of my life on your altar, and watch for fire to descend (Psalm 5:3 *The Message*).

The Holy Spirit indwelling us does incredible things. Like Moses, we know we are on holy ground. Like Paul, being blinded gives us a single vision for the rest of our lives. Like Peter, denial and fear are transformed into proclamation and boldness.

Let us pray that His face will shine upon us and that we may be saved (Psalm 80:7). Ordinary things—turned around by the supernatural touch of a Holy God—then become extraordinary.

John wrote, "My little children, I am writing these things to you that you may not sin. And if anyone sins, we have an Advocate with the Father, Jesus Christ the righteous" (1 John 2:1 NASV). The One who walks beside us is the Holy Spirit. He was sent to stand beside us. "The one who says he abides in Him ought himself to walk in the same manner as He walked" (1 John 2:6 NASV). We are to walk the way He walked and do the work He has called us to do.

Paul says we are to be filled with the Spirit to all fullness (Eph. 3:19). A story is told about several pastors who met to discuss inviting noted evangelist D. L. Moody to speak at an upcoming crusade. After one man highly recommended Dr. Moody, another said, "It sounds like D. L. Moody has a monopoly on the Holy Spirit!"

"Oh no," the first speaker replied, "Dr. Moody doesn't have a monopoly on the Holy

Spirit. The Holy Spirit has a monopoly on Dr. Moody!"

3

Melt Me

The Holy Spirit—Our Power

> You are the potter, I am the clay,
> Melt me and mold me.
> This is what I pray.

Eddie Espinosa, "Change My Heart, O God" © 1982
Mercy/Vineyard Publishers

> "But now, O Lord, You are our
> Father; We are the clay, and You are
> our potter; And all we are the work
> of Your hand" (Isa. 64:8 NKJV).

The Holy Spirit:
The Transforming Agent

A potter shapes the clay. In the hands of the
Master Potter, our lives are formed and
molded to be all that He desires us to be. I'm
told that potters often destroy a pot in the
process, throwing it back onto the potter's
wheel, then molding it again and again to
achieve the desired shape. It seems like harsh
treatment, but not in the potter's mind—he
desires the best. The potter knows what he
wants the vessel to be, just as the Master Potter
knows who He wants us to be.

*So here's what I want you to do, God help-
ing you: Take your everyday, ordinary life—
your sleeping, eating, going to-work, and walk-
ing-around life—and place it before God as an
offering. Embracing what God does for you is
the best thing you can do for Him. Don't
become so well-adjusted to your culture that you
fit into it without even thinking. Instead, fix
your attention on God. You'll be changed from
the inside out (Rom.12:1, 2 The Message).*

What a transformation! God's Spirit
changes us from the inside out. Surely this is
the measure of a Spirit-filled life.

On many retreat weekends at which
I speak, the worship leader sometimes leads
the audience to sing the chorus, "Change My
Heart, O God":

*You are the potter, I am the clay,
Melt me and mold me. This is what I pray.*

Each time I sing this my spirit cries out
within me, "Please, Father, please! Melt me
and mold me!" I'm thankful when we sing
that chorus—the Holy Spirit knows I need to
be reminded that our gathering is about Him,
not about me. It's about His melting and
molding my heart.

I beg Him, "Please, Father, as You pour
Your Holy Spirit through me, touch my own
heart as you touch the hearts of the listeners."

The work of the Holy Spirit is to melt our
hearts so He can mold our lives. As our lives
are molded by the Spirit, we begin to look

more like Him. Our lives give testimony to His power in us, drawing others to Christ. A pastor at Oak Grove United Methodist Church in Decatur, Georgia, shared this story, The Power of Forgiveness, given to him by fellow minister Terry Phillips:

There was once a Methodist bishop on the West Coast by the name of Donald H. Tippett. He was a good man and a splendid preacher. His face was slightly disfigured and one eye looked a little strange. Many did not know his story until after his death. As a young minister in New York, Donald Tippett served a church on the lower East Side. He was working late one Saturday when three young men entered the church and beat him brutally with brass knuckles. When they finished, he was unconscious with one eye gouged out. Thinking he was dead, the young men jammed him behind a wall radiator and left the church. A while later, Gertrude Ederle, the professional channel swimmer, came to the church where she was teaching a lifesaving course. She discovered the minister and immediately summoned help. For a long time Donald lay in a hospital bed, hovering between life and death, but he did eventually recover.

Meanwhile, the three thugs were apprehended. One was later executed for another crime he had committed. Donald Tippett befriended the other two, treating them like his own sons. One of them responded, the other

As you and I obey the Holy Spirit in our lives, we allow the Spirit freedom to be the finger of God, pointing out to us what God is doing.

did not. *The one who responded was helped to go to college and finally to medical school.*

Somewhere in the US today, there is a distinguished eye surgeon who owes everything he is and has to one person who believed in and practiced the principle of forgiveness—Donald Tippett.

What a testimony to the work of the Holy Spirit in Donald Tippett's life. The Holy Spirit in him allowed Donald to forgive—and even more, to restore. A watching world saw a man that looked much like God in his actions toward the three who had almost killed him. These young men were given the opportunity to embrace God's love through the power of forgiveness.

During the reign of Oliver Cromwell, the British government began to run low on silver coins. Lord Cromwell sent his men to the local cathedrals to see if they could find any precious metals. The men reported, "The only silver we could find was the statues of the saints standing in the corners," to which the radical soldier and statesman of England replied, "Good. We'll melt down the saints and put them into circulation!"

Just imagine—melted saints circulating through the mainstream of humanity, bringing value to everyday life. Not the saints who are dressed up in three-piece-suits or shiny silk dresses, comfortably seated on a padded pew every Sunday. No, Jesus desires that we be "melted down" saints in the marketplaces of life—on campuses, in shops, in corporate offices, in homes, on the streets—everywhere there are people. We are not to be statues in the church—shiny and polished. We are to be melted down—as in "poured into"—moving through our marketplace as saints empowered by the power of the Holy Spirit.

The summer of 1974, while we were on the faculty at Samford University in Birmingham, Alabama, Bob was invited by Walt Disney World in Orlando, Florida, to direct the Kids of the Kingdom in the Summer College Workshop Program. Every afternoon, and for the final event every night, a big parade takes place at Walt Disney World. People line the streets early to get a good spot. The employees put on their costumes or performance outfits and march in the parade.

A man once stopped Walt Disney and asked him, "Why do you have a parade every day?" Walt answered, "When you march in the parade, you see the eyes of the people watching the parade, and you remember why we have a parade." A parade has the kind of impact that draws the crowd into the parade, if only in their minds, for that magical moment when everyone celebrates.

God sent His Son, Jesus Christ, to march in the "Parade of Life." Everywhere Jesus went, He marched with a purpose and intent given Him by God. On His way to the cross, Jesus ministered to and called followers. He ministered through God's power and for God's glory. As you and I obey the Holy Spirit in our lives, we allow the Spirit freedom to be the finger of God, pointing out to us what God is doing. In the Father's world, this "parade" is about the Holy Spirit drawing us in as He works to melt and mold us, making us look like Jesus while preparing us for Kingdom life.

The Holy Spirit's Work Always Points to Jesus

Some time ago I spoke at a student conference in New Mexico. I had spoken several times during the week, and was bringing the final message on Thursday night. I don't remember the exact message, but I'm almost positive that I was calling the student generation to follow God's call upon their lives—to make an impact on the world for the Kingdom of God.

The plan for the evening was that after I spoke, I would step back from the podium while a dramatic presentation on the cross would be made. I would then return to the podium to extend the evening's invitation. I am constantly amazed to see how the Holy Spirit will bring elements of worship together—music, proclamation, and drama— to communicate the gospel. I marvel as the Holy Spirit works through these media.

The drama was magnificent and my heart was deeply touched, my tears flowing freely. In the midst of the drama as I watched intently, a young woman touched my arm, asking if she could speak with me. I wanted to stay where I was to see the conclusion of the drama, but her tears drew me. She said that she wanted to know Christ. I thought, "I have to watch the drama, at the conclusion I am to give the invitation." But I began to visit

with the young woman about her relationship
to the Father. When I realized it was time for
me to come and invite students to the altar, I
excused myself and promised her I would be
right back. I then simply invited the students
to come and accept God's call on their lives.
Student ministers came to the front—waiting
to receive students. As I moved away from the
podium I sensed the Spirit of God moving
across the room. I moved back to the side
stairs and sat by the young woman, continuing
to share God's word and showing her how to
accept Christ as her personal Savior.

She then prayed with me to receive Christ.
After we prayed, we walked together out the
back door. I made my way back to my room,
feeling a need to be alone with God to
ponder the moving of His Holy Spirit.

The next morning at breakfast, several student ministers spoke with me about how
God's Spirit fell fresh on that service, saying
they had not seen students respond like that in
a long time—students on their knees and
faces, praying before God. Some remarked,
"It was a fresh wind of God's Spirit." Though
I was aware of the Holy Spirit's presence, I did
not see the work done by the Spirit except in
that young woman who had accepted Christ.
I was only told about it later. How precious
that the Spirit did not allow me to see it. I
might have thought I had done it!

Write this down: *When the Holy Spirit
works, He always points to Jesus, never to a person.*
Thus He gives God the Glory. His work is to
point us to the Father, not to people. We are
sometimes prone to explain what happened

If you can explain it, you can take credit for it. If you can't explain it, you can be sure the Holy Spirit is working.

and how we had a part in it. Even when the Spirit chooses to work through us in a situation, after the event we will leave and go home. But the Spirit will continue to work. It is His work, not ours!

If you can explain it, you can take credit for it. If you can't explain it, you can be sure the Holy Spirit is working.

The work of the Holy Spirit is to glorify God. And we best not try to take any of God's glory. "Now when they saw the boldness of Peter and John, and perceived that they were uneducated and untrained men, they marveled. And they realized they had been with Jesus" (Acts 4:13). Oswald Chambers writes: "Complete abandon to the love of Christ is the one thing that bears fruit in the life, and it will always leave the impression of the holiness and of the power of God...never our personal holiness."

We are humbled when we recognize the working of the Holy Spirit in and through us. When the Spirit chooses us as a vessel to point to Jesus, we become the *fruit bearers*, not the fruit producers. The Holy Spirit produces the fruit, to the glory of God.

I was speaking at a women's conference in the fall of 1998, when two women asked to speak with me. They both told me their stories. Unknown to me, they had been college students in attendance at that student conference in New Mexico many years earlier, (attending the conference I referred to earlier in this chapter).

Both had felt the call of God in their lives and had responded to the Holy Spirit at that

Thursday night session. They told me, "We were there on our knees before God that night, surrendering our lives to God for ministry, as you shared your life verse, Ephesians 3:20, 'Now unto Him who is able to do exceedingly abundantly above all that we ask or think, according to the power that works in us, to Him be glory, in the church by Christ Jesus to all generations forever and ever.'" Holy! Holy! Holy!

Be reminded that it was the power of the Holy Spirit—not me—that drew these beautiful young women. And it is the Spirit of God that works in their lives today as they serve along with their husbands in ministry. When the Holy Spirit works He transforms lives, making fit vessels for kingdom work. "He is the potter, I am the clay! Melt me and mold me, This is what I pray."

The Holy Spirit's Power and Authority

My friend and mentor, Pitts Hughes, tells about the time she was a chaplain to student nurses at a hospital in Birmingham, Alabama. Tired and discouraged after a long day's work, she threw her things on the bed and said aloud, "For all the good I'm doing here, I might as well go home." A conversation followed between Pitts and Dowella, a small, frail cleaning woman who worked in the dorm.

Dowella asked Pitts, "Who's inside of you?"

"God," answered Pitts, ". . . a God of love, self-control, and power."

We go through exactly what Christ goes through. If we go through the hard times with him, then we're certainly going to go through the good times with him! (Rom. 8:15–17 The Message)

Dowella looked straight into Pitts's eyes and said, "If God's Spirit is inside of you, and He's all power, ain't you got power?"

You see, the Holy Spirit living inside of us is the power available to us. Dowella's idea may not have been stated the best way grammatically, but it is profound theology. Dowella understood the person and work of the Holy Spirit. Jesus said, "I will pray the Father, and He shall give you another Comforter, that He may abide with you for ever; even the Spirit of truth; whom the world cannot receive, because it seeth him not, neither knoweth him: but ye know Him; for He dwelleth with you, and shall be in you" (John 14: 16-17 KJV). When Jesus raised Lazarus from the dead, He prayed, "I know you will do this, but I am asking on their account so they will believe You did it." Thus He showed His followers that God receives the glory.

The Spirit is the power
The Christian is the instrument.
The instrument without the power is useless.
The power without the instrument
is inoperable.

This resurrection life you received from God is not a timid, grave-tending life. It's adventurously expectant, greeting God with a childlike "What's next, Papa?" God's Spirit touches our spirits and confirms who we really are. We know who He is, and we know who we are: Father and children.

And we know we are going to get what's coming to us—an unbelievable inheritance!

We go through exactly what Christ goes through. If we go through the hard times with him, then we're certainly going to go through the good times with him!"(Rom. 8:15–17 *The Message*). We can live like Christ only in the Holy Spirit's power. We ask, "What's next, Papa?" as we face our everyday events, living as instruments of God with the Holy Spirit's power.

When my phone rang one day I immediately recognized the voices—Ruth Fennel and Ida Richards, two delightful older saints of God living in Atlanta, Georgia who prayed for me as I've traveled. Ruth has now gone home to be with the Father. Each month I would provide Ruth and Miss Ida with my travel schedule, and they would pray for my speaking and travels every day. Of course, following each trip they would immediately call to ask what God had done through us! Our sharing began a journey that was new to me.

That particular day as we shared on the phone about a concern in my life, Ruth began to talk with the Heavenly Father about the matter. Then, a moment later, she resumed our conversation. I was pleasantly refreshed. Of course the Holy Spirit can be heard over long-distance phone lines! Ruth was so comfortable with the Source of power in her life that she was in constant conversation with the One who Empowers. Prayer was her breath, and she prayed constantly. What happened on the phone that day should not have surprised me. God, the God of Abraham, Moses, and Joshua, lives with His people. This God promises, "I will never

desert you, nor will I ever forsake you" (Heb.
13:5 NASV). This promise in Hebrews is
affirmed three different ways:

1. Never will I leave you
2. Never will I forsake you
3. No, not ever

Right now, get your Bible and find John
14:15–21. Write your name everywhere the
word *you* appears. Then celebrate!

I was thinking recently about my last visit
with Ruth before her death. I was told she
could not speak because of her condition, that
I could not get close to her because of her
infectious condition, and that she would prob-
ably not recognize me. My heart ached as I
saw my friend in such a frail condition.

I leaned down to her and whispered,
"Ruth. It's Esther." She opened her eyes and
smiled, and her mouth formed the words "I
pray for you." What a treasure was mine that
day—that for a brief moment she knew who I
was, and she reminded me of her prayers for
my life. The power of the Holy Spirit is
released through our prayers.

We need to live expectantly of what the
Holy Spirit is going to do in our lives. He will
place on our hearts the message He wants us to
speak to the world in which we live. Stop right
now and write this down: *God's Holy Spirit is
within me. And I am within Him.*

Jesus told us that He would be with us and
that God would be within us. He promised
never to leave us alone. He walks through life
with us. He is our Companion. He cares
about us—what we eat, what we wear, where
we go—everything about us. Imagine

beginning each day with Jesus inviting you to go everywhere He goes:

"I'm going to the bank this morning, Esther. Please ride with me. We might see Alicia, the bank teller with whom you are making friends. She's one of mine, too.

I am meeting some friends for lunch and I believe you would enjoy the conversation about last week's Bible study on the Holy Spirit. Please join me. The women's committee is meeting this afternoon to plan the upcoming retreat. The prayer group has been praying that My presence will be felt all weekend, so let's join their meeting and prayer time."

Jesus invites me to do everything with Him. How revolutionary to live this way! Try it! We are the tabernacles of God. He dwells within each of us. He wishes to take our ordinary days and ordinary circumstances and put His supernatural power into our lives. Act on it! Believe it! Live it!

The Holy Spirit:
Working through Abandoned Lives

In Acts 4:13 Luke writes: "Now when they saw the boldness of Peter and John, and perceived that they were uneducated and untrained men, they marveled. And they realized they had been with Jesus." My passion today is to call women to live passionately and intentionally for Christ—to live lives that are abandoned to Christ. I find that today's younger generation desires to touch the world for Christ. They may not be interested in a denomination or organization, but they are

Jesus' death would move worship from a place—the temple—to a person—Truth. Jesus Christ has made our bodies His dwelling place. Praise God!

interested in an authentic life in Christ. They want to understand our relationship to Christ and whether it makes a difference. They want to touch the world in a significant way. Jesus led the way. We find Him making a difference in unexpected places and unplanned circumstances. He would relate well to Generation Xers, Boomers, Busters, and Bridgers!

Let's recall the conversation between Jesus and the Samaritan woman. She explained to Jesus, "Our fathers worshiped on this mountain and you Jews say that in Jerusalem is the place where one ought to worship" (John 4:20 NKJV).

Jesus answered, "But the hour is coming, and now is, when the true worshippers will worship the Father in spirit and truth; for the Father is seeking such to worship Him. God is Spirit, and those who worship Him must worship in spirit and truth" (John 4:23, 24 NKJV).

Jesus' death would move worship from a place—the temple—to a person—Truth. Jesus Christ has made our bodies His dwelling place. Praise God!

The disciples—yes, even His own disciples, like us—didn't get it. They marveled that He was speaking to a woman. Perhaps we should be asking, "Who marvels at the company you keep, the friends you make, and the places you go to share His Truth?" There are people everywhere waiting to hear the Truth: Chicago, New York City, Boise, Phoenix, Charleston, Miami, Houston, San Francisco, Jakarta, Hong Kong, Rio de Janeiro, Nairobi, Paris. They are waiting. Will you choose to

be abandoned to Christ? Perhaps we should
follow the example of Ray Bakke. Ray and
his family deliberately choose to live in a
racially mixed Chicago neighborhood marked
by violence. On their block alone, seventeen
nations are represented. In its school system of
470,000 students, fifty-three nations are represented. Forty percent of the students come
from single-parent homes. Over half are
ethnic minorities. Ray says that he and his
family purposely choose to live in the community to witness for Jesus. Today, Ray's son
Brian serves in the inner city as a
missionary—abandoned to Christ in a difficult
city!

Christ asks us to penetrate our culture
with the gospel. He wants us to be in the
world, but not of the world.

Consider what could happen if Christians
chose schools, neighborhoods, and workplaces
for the purpose of sharing the gospel rather
than because of their earning power!

I was intrigued by a seventy-nine-year-old
woman I met one summer. Carmen was serving as housemother for North American
Mission Board summer missionaries in
Daytona Beach, Florida. I asked Carmen why
she had volunteered for work at age seventy-
nine.

"Esther, it all started when I was sixty-four
years old. I read an article in *Royal Service*
magazine (now *Missions Mosaic*) urging
Christians of any age or circumstance to go as
Christ commanded. As I read the article I
tried to decide where I could go. The Lord
began to speak to me through this article, and

I opened my Bible and sought His direction.
He first led me to Genesis 12:1: "The Lord
said to Abraham, 'Leave your country, your
people and your father's household and go to
the land I will show you'" (NIV). Then He
led me to Jeremiah 8:20: "The harvest is past,
the summer has ended, and we are not saved"
(NIV). The next verse in my devotion was
Lamentations 1:12: "Is it nothing to you, all
you who pass by? Look around and see"
(NIV). I felt called, and that feeling has never
left me. I know it's true, for I couldn't do
what I do if I didn't feel called.

Carmen decided she was too old to be on
a payroll, but not too old to work. She has
since worked in missions in Arizona,
Pennsylvania, and Florida.

"Carmen," I said, "you live in Georgia.
What do you do with your house while you
are gone on these missions appointments?"
Carmen smiled and said, "I just lock it up and
say, 'Here it is, Lord. Take care of it 'till I get
back! You told me to go.'" Carmen has
abandoned herself to Christ. She added, "I
have never said 'no' to anything God has
asked me to do."

Ethel is another person serving through
the Holy Spirit's power. One Wednesday
night at prayer meeting, the Lord told her she
needed to take food and money to a certain
family in the community. When she arrived at
the home, she found the family in tears. The
mother was ill, and all their money had been
spent on medical bills. There was no money
left for gas or food. The family had just finished praying, asking God to send help.

Ethel was the help that God sent to them. The Holy Spirit spoke to her and told her to go, and she was obedient. She later said to me, "I was the person God needed to answer someone else's prayer, and that alone is reason enough to listen to the Holy Spirit." Think of it, precious sisters in Christ: Through the Spirit's power, you may be the person God will use to answer someone's prayer—a "melted-down saint"!

Since I met Kay in Atlanta several years ago, I have discovered she really does live by Ephesians 3:20. Kay resides in an upper-middle-class suburb of Atlanta, where she is involved in the youth ministry of her church. The youth wanted to make a difference in their city, and decided to invite homeless people from an inner-city shelter to their annual Christmas program. Kay arranged for the youth to provide transportation to and from the church. In addition, the youth would fix a meal for the persons attending.

For most of the youth, this was their first contact with homeless people. Kay recalls, "It was a freezing day, about eighteen degrees. We had a nice meal, enjoyed the service, gave presents to our guests, and then returned the people to the shelter.

When they arrived at the shelter, however, the doors were still locked. It was not yet time for the shelter to open! The last ones off the bus were a woman with two small children and a three-week-old infant." Kay said to her husband, "We can't let them off in this cold!" Turning to the woman, she asked, "If we let you off, where will you go?" The woman

Think of it, precious sisters in Christ: Through the Spirit's power, you may be the person God will use to answer someone's prayer—a "melted-down saint"!

answered, "I'll just wander the streets until the shelter opens." Kay and her husband went and banged on the doors of the shelter until someone came and agreed to let this family in early.

Kay continued to think about this family. She recalls, "The Lord just touched me. I had never seen or felt anything like this before. I went home thinking, 'it is almost Christmas and these people are living on the streets all day long—even with a baby.' " She asked her family, "How would you like to invite that mother and her children to spend Christmas with us?"

Her family agreed. Kay contacted the family at the shelter and made arrangements for them to spend Christmas day with her family.

When Kay went to pick up the woman and children, the woman asked her if they could also include the woman's husband. Kay asked, "You mean you have a husband, and you live in this shelter?"

The woman responded, "Yes, but my husband lives in the men's shelter. We can't stay together." You can guess where Kay drove next. After picking up the husband, they went by the hospital to check on the baby, who had become ill. The baby was well enough to be released, but not well enough to go to the shelter. As the family stood there trying to decide what to do, Kay thought to herself, "I do not know these people."

But aloud she said, "They can all stay at my house!" Kay discovered that the family had come from Missouri to Atlanta to seek a better

job and a better way of life. They had lived in
a trailer for a few months, but after the birth of
their third child they were evicted because the
trailer park allowed only four persons per unit.
From there they had gone to the downtown
shelters because there was no where else they
could go.

The husband had been looking for work,
but so far had no offers. Kay learned that the
couple's situation was complicated because
they had married early in life, had no formal
education past high school, and had a lot of
obstacles to overcome. Kay offered to keep
the children in her home while the couple
looked for work. So for two weeks during
Christmas vacation the homeless family
became Kay's extended family!

Before long, the husband found a job. A
member of Kay's church provided them a
rent-free apartment until they could get back
on their feet financially. Other members provided furniture, clothing for the children, and
food for the pantry.

When Kay returned to the shelter to pick
up the family's belongings, the director
expressed gratitude for what Kay's family had
done. Kay responded, "We haven't done
much—not compared to you and your staff.
You're the ones who work here seven nights a
week providing a place for these people to
stay. We've really done very little."

To this the director replied, "If all the
churches in our city would do just a little, we
could take care of the homeless in Atlanta. It's
the little things that really count." What a
message! If we will abandon ourselves to the

Here were high-school-aged young women— abandoned to the power of the Holy Spirit and meeting the needs of others in Christ's name. Can we do less?

power of the Holy Spirit within us, we could change the world!

We are to be God's hands
- at day care centers,
- in the job bank,
- in the car,
- at the shelter,
- in the food line, and
- on the street.

As we feed others, we are feeding Him. When we clothe others, we clothe Him. When we find others a job or a home, we are doing this for Him. What an incredible opportunity the Father gives us as He clothes us in His power.

A high school girl's mission organization traveled north one summer to conduct a "Big A Club." A Big A Club is like Vacation Bible School—a way of teaching children about Jesus—children who have had little if any contact with a church. The weather was unusually chilly for that time of the year. One of the children who came to the Big A Club sat in the circle shivering. "Where's your jacket?" one of the teenage girls asked.

"I ain't got none," the little girl replied.

The girls went to their leader: "We've got to find a store and buy her a jacket!" The leader thought to herself, "They can't possibly afford to do that!" She prayed, "God, what should I do?"

As she and the girls drove back to camp from a grocery shopping trip, they noticed a sign indicating a garage sale in progress. She pulled off the road, and the girls got out in search for a jacket. They found a jacket that needed just a little mending. That evening the teenagers mended the jacket, and the next day they lovingly presented it to the girl. Only then did the girls realize that the other children were also shivering in the cold as well.

That night, these precious teens plotted what they could do. They took some canvas tarp from their camping supplies, and cut it into triangles, making canvas shawls to wrap around the children for warmth. The young women realized they could not tell these children about the love of God while the children sat there shivering. Their physical needs had to be met before their spiritual needs could be addressed. Here were high-school-aged young women— abandoned to the power of the Holy Spirit and meeting the needs of others in Christ's name.

Can we do less?

The Needs

One of the dark sides of life in America is the abuse of women, children, and the elderly. I discovered this firsthand when I volunteered in a South Florida shelter for abused women. Many Christians have no concept of the hurt and fear that is prevalent in the world today.

I didn't do much while there; I just listened with my heart. Those women needed to know that someone cares!

One church in the Midwest has started a ministry for abused children. In 1976, there were 170 convictions for child abuse in this

Gouger said, "American children now are more likely to be murdered, poor, pregnant, drug-dependent, or incarcerated than the children of any other industrialized country in the world."

Midwestern city. By 1981, the number had grown to more than eight thousand. In cities across our nation, statistics like these keep increasing.

This city, as well as the church located there, became aware of this growing problem. Social workers in the community needed four thousand volunteers to assist with the needs of abused children, but they were able to secure only three hundred. The local child abuse agency came to the church for help.

The agency asked the church for volunteers willing to spend two or three hours a day working with abused children. Volunteers would spend time with the children, play games with them, help with homework, and just be their friends.

The church responded, saying, "We are Christians, and as we help these children with their homework and other things, we will share Jesus Christ with them."

The agency responded, "We don't care. We want these children to receive love, guidance, and support. If you want to share Christianity with them, then share it."

I recently learned of a program called "Kids Hope USA." This ministry reaches out to kids at risk through a mentoring program. Dr. Virgil Gouger is president of this ministry. He shared about the ministry on the radio program Focus on the Family. Gouger said, "American children now are more likely to be murdered, poor, pregnant, drug-dependent, or incarcerated than the children of any other industrialized country in the world."

- Children from birth to three years old are the most neglected children in the world.
- In the US a child is fifteen times more likely to be murdered than in Ireland.
- A teen in the US is killed every five hours.
- A preschool child is killed every thirteen hours.
- The suicide rate for kids under age fourteen has jumped 75 percent from 1989 to 1999.

(Hope for the Children, panel, CT17022461, Focus on the Family radio program)

Kids Hope USA enlists and trains, through local churches, volunteers who will commit to one hour with one child each week. The child is recommended by his or her teacher. Parental permission is granted. The school system reports that after two, sixty-minute mentoring sessions teachers can see an improvement in attitude, grades, and self-esteem.

Not only are the children changed, but churches report that they have earned a positive reputation in their community. A statement appeared in the media, "It's the first evidence of authentic Christian living we have seen in years."

Most churches are event- or program-oriented. The church promotes programs for members birth through old age. The event or program is the church's entry point for many people. Our culture has come to expect this of churches. What our culture doesn't expect is that the church will go to the jails, high-rise

Jesus is inviting you to go with Him.

apartment buildings, or shelters. We should not give up the wonderful programs in our churches. But we should look at the needs of society, and develop strategies that will bring the church to the people.

Consider these opportunities:

- *A Christian lawyer helps couples work toward reconciliation rather than divorce, and shares about the reconciling love of God.*
- *A physician helps his patients not only with their physical sickness but helps them to understand their spiritual sickness as well.*
- *Christian schoolteachers volunteer one afternoon a week to help illiterate adults learn how to read and write.*
- *Professional workers tutor international students at a local university. Many of these students come from countries that do not allow missionaries. After graduation the students return to their native countries taking the gospel with them.*

We have relegated for too long the priestly role to the paid staff of our churches. Every child of God is called to be a priest before God. If God has not called us to a distant mission field, then we can use our professions and other skills to share Christ right here where we work and live. As we work in the marketplace, let us recognize the needs of the world and seek to make a difference in Christ's name.

If we are to reclaim our world for Christ, we must get outside the church, letting missions become our way of life.

Ask these questions of yourself:
- *What are the gifts God has given me?*
- *What are the needs in my world?*
- *What can I do to make a difference?*

Jesus invites you to go with Him as He enters the mission field right where you live:
- *Join a support group for alcohol and drug abusers, or other persons experiencing problems,*
- *Become a Big Sister or Big Brother to a child from a broken home,*
- *Invite a non-believer into your home as an offer of friendship,*
- *Provide job counseling and training to unemployed persons,*
- *Provide support to women in crisis pregnancies,*
- *Tutor latch-key children, offering them a safe after school environment,*
- *Coach or participate in an inner-city sports league.*

Jesus is inviting you to go with Him.

4

Mold Me

The Holy Spirit—Our Presence

Surely the presence of the Lord
is in this place,
I can feel His mighty power
and His grace
I can feel the brush of angels' wings,
I see glory on each face,
Surely the presence of the Lord
is in this place.

"Surely the Presence of the Lord is in this Place"
© 1977 Lanny Wolfe Music/ASCAP (Admin. By ICG).
All rights reserved. Used by permission.

One of the "winds" that the Holy Spirit often
uses in my life is that I hear music before I
speak. I'm not a singer, but I have a heart for
music and for singing. My heart sings to the
Father. In January 1997, Daytona Beach,
Florida was the site of a musical experience
for senior adults planned by my husband. Kurt
Kaiser, a wonderfully gentle songwriter, wrote
a musical just for the occasion and was there
to teach the musical.

Also on the program was George Beverly
Shea, the renowned solo vocalist on the Billy
Graham team. What a delightful two days it
was! As Mr. Shea stepped up to sing "How
Great Thou Art," I felt as if we'd just reached

heaven. What a gentle spirit this man has. He shared with us over dinner that his solo work on the Graham team was not so much for the audience as it was for Mr. Graham. "Billy always asks me to sing just before he preaches. He says it's for his heart," Mr. Shea told us.

I was at a meeting recently in Alabama where Alicia W. Garcia led in worship. Beth Moore and I were part of the speaking team. What a powerful worship leader Alicia is. Speaking on the theme "Empowered," I began the service by talking about the person and work of the Holy Spirit and the fact that when the Spirit works He always points to Jesus—never to Esther Burroughs or Beth Moore—but always to Jesus. Then Alicia got up and sang her solo.

Following Alicia, Beth stepped to the platform and, in her energetic way, said, "I was on my knees this morning, telling God I needed an hour to bring my message and they'd only given me twenty-five minutes. Then Esther gets up and gives the first half of my message, and Alicia sings the next part, and so here I go with the last part." The women laughed. Beth and I looked at each other, acknowledging the power of the Spirit to lead each of us when we had not talked with each other about what we were to share that day. The Spirit of God moved in Beth as she proclaimed His message, and then she called the women to pray at the altar.

As Alicia said to me later, "You could feel the Holy Spirit moving from the back of the room to the front, making His presence known."

*Dwight L.
Moody once
made the
statement:
"Every work of
God can be
traced to some
kneeling form."*

Paul says, "I bow my knees before the Father of our Lord Jesus Christ, from whom the whole family in heaven and earth derives its name" (Eph. 3:14–15 NASV).

Surely one place to acknowledge the presence of the Holy Spirit is on our knees. Dwight L. Moody once made the statement: "Every work of God can be traced to some kneeling form."

We live in a very busy and diverse world. Yet Jesus said, "My kingdom is not of this world" (John 18:36 KJV).

Oswald Chambers, in *My Utmost for His Highest*, wrote these words:

The great enemy to the Lord Jesus Christ in the present day is the conception of practical work that has not come from the New Testament, but from the systems of the world in which endless energy and activities are insisted upon, but no private life with God. The emphasis is put on the wrong thing. Jesus said, 'The kingdom of God cometh not with observation, for lo, the kingdom of God is within you,' a hidden, obscure thing. An active Christian worker too often lives in the shop window.

It is the innermost of the innermost that reveals the power of the life.[1]

The time I spend in the presence of God through prayer releases the power of the Holy Spirit to work in me, empowering me to work for His kingdom. I am reminded of two scriptures: "Greater is He that is in you, than he that is in the world" (1 John 4:4 KJV); and "Most assuredly, I say to you, he who believes in Me, the works that I do he will do also; and greater works than these he will do, because I go to my Father. And whatever you ask in My name, that will I do, that the Father may be glorified in the Son. If you ask anything in My name, I will do it. If you love Me, keep My commandments. And I will pray the Father, and He will give you another Helper, that He may abide with you forever, even the Spirit of Truth, whom the world cannot receive, because it neither sees Him nor knows Him; but you know Him, for He dwells with you and will be in you" (John 14:12–17 NKJV).

The story is told of a historic radio broadcast in 1930 that was to be given by King George of England as he addressed the International Arms Control Summit. At just the time the broadcast was to begin, a technician tripped over a cable in the New York studio, causing it to break. The CBS chief engineer, Harold Vivian, looked for something to patch the cable, but found nothing. He took one end of the severed cable in one hand and the other end in his other hand, making that historic broadcast possible: his body served as the connecting power. The King's message was carried to the people through a power that coursed through a single human being.

You and I are to be the vessels through which the Holy Spirit's power courses.

In the verses above (John 14:12–17), our Lord unfolds the unique secret of Christianity,

This means that what you and I do in the power of the Holy Spirit will not fade away, but will remain forever.

the aspect of life that has been called "the exchanged life."

Ray C. Stedman writes in his book *Talking With My Father,* "We live the life of another, or more accurately, another lives His life through us." Stedman points out that a Christian's work is borrowed activity, the basis of a Christian's prayer is borrowed authority; and the secret of Christian living is borrowed deity.

Stedman writes:

The risen Christ will do through us greater works than He did as the incarnate Christ living among men! Do you see the difference? That's an incredible promise—but it makes absolute biblical sense. It is not we but He who will do these greater works—and He will perform them through us. It is not activity that makes a difference in the world. It is borrowed activity—work that we borrow from Christ, and which He performs on earth through us.[2]

Remember Jesus' last discourse with His disciples in the upper room? He said, "You did not choose me, but I chose you and appointed you that you should go and bear fruit and that your fruit shall remain, that whatever you ask the Father in My name He may give you" (John 15:16 NKJV). This means that what you and I do in the power of the Holy Spirit will not fade away, but will remain forever.

Stedman continues:

It is His work in us. A Christian's true work

*is borrowed activity. It is never on our own,
and when we begin to think it is, we defeat
every possibility of success. We sabotage the
work of the Holy Spirit.*

Wow! In our walk with the Father, *faith* is
the operative word. Sisters in Christ, walk in
the Spirit of faith.

Stedman also says, "Just as the basis of a
Christian's work is borrowed activity, so the
basis of a Christian's prayer is borrowed
authority." Jesus said "And whatever you ask
in My name, that I will do, that the Father
may be glorified in the Son. If you ask anything in My name, I will do it" (John 14:13,
14 NKJV).

I often say to my audiences, "He has given
you His name. . .use it!"

When I married Bob, he gave me his
name. I've added it to mine, and have been
using it for forty-plus years. This gives me his
authority—it protects me and gives me a certain status. With his name, he gave me his
love, and I accept his authority in using his
name. The Father gave you His name, but it
comes with conditions.

Stedman writes:

*This promise cannot be limitless, it is condi-
tional. We dare not miss the real implications
of that all-important, twice-stated clause, "in
my name." To ask something in Christ's name
means to ask by His authority. It means to ask
on the basis of His character according to the
merit of His work, and by the power and right*

*that He has personally given to us. This means
that Jesus has lent His authority to us, giving
us the authority to pray according to His
authority, which we have borrowed.*[3]

I use my husband's name and authority
when writing checks or signing deeds. In
receiving his name I accept this authority and
privilege. Remember that the Holy Spirit
always points to Jesus, to bring glory to His
father, and He does this by lending His
authority to us. So when we pray, we are
asking by virtue of His authority and in His
name, according to His will, that God may be
glorified.

Stedman further teaches us:

*The secret to a Christian's life is borrowed
deity. John 14:15-17, "If you love me, you
will do what I command. I will ask the
Father, and He will give you another
Counselor, the Spirit of truth, to be with you
forever . . . you know Him, for He lives with
you and will be in you."*

What a staggering truth! He is the one who
makes Himself at home in my life. He is the
one who fills us with the fullness of God. The
Holy Spirit makes Himself at home in you.

In the August 1989, issue of *the
COMMISSION* magazine, Foreign Mission
Board president Keith Parks tells of visiting a
shop in Ho Chi Minh city (formerly Saigon).
In the shop Dr. Parks met a Vietnamese man
who, while training as a pilot, had visited

several places in the United States. He had
even flown for the United States Air Force.
After the fall of South Vietnam, the man had
spent time in a Vietnamese reeducation camp.
The man shared some of the circumstances of
his life and his desperation to find a better life.
He told Parks he was very poor. They had
trouble communicating with each other, but
Parks discovered that this man had never heard
of Jesus Christ! He had lived in three different
Southern states, yet had never once been
invited to a church.

Dr. Parks recalls, "Trying to communicate
in simple terms, I began describing the fact that
his circumstances, which he had defined as
being desperate and unsatisfactory, could be
changed. 'I personally cannot help you,' I said.
'However, I know someone who can. His name
is Jesus Christ.' Instantly, the man responded,
'What is His address?' " [4]

This question stunned Dr. Parks. The true
answer to this question was like a kick in the
stomach. The actual, practical address of Jesus
Christ is every Christian! Wherever we live,
wherever we work, wherever we go, Jesus
Christ goes with us and is within us.

If the Spirit has loaned us His authority,
His activity, and His deity, then why do we
live lives that are empty of joy and power? It
may be that He has taken up a position in you
through salvation, but does not have full possession of you.

Maybe it is time you "borrowed" Him and
His power. As you and I come under the
obedience of the Holy Spirit, we will discover
that indeed we are under His direction.

The actual, practical address of Jesus Christ is every Christian! Wherever we live, wherever we work, wherever we go, Jesus Christ goes with us and is within us.

I believe this generation longs to see Christians as persons with an authentic resemblance to Christ—who have the power to make others thirsty for the living water.

The Holy Spirit's daily leadership in our lives is the defining characteristic of every disciple. I know no finer way to define the relationship with the Spirit than through daily prayer and Bible study. I have recently been working through Beth Moore's study on Paul's life, *To Live is Christ*. Acts 20:22 tells of Paul having been "compelled by the Spirit" to go on to Jerusalem, even though trouble lay ahead. Once Paul discerned the will of God, nothing could stop him. When the ship was ready to sail, Paul's friends accompanied him to the ship. Beth writes,

Can you imagine what a sight this scene must have been for others to behold? Men, women, and children kneeling in the sand praying with one heart and mind for the apostle and his beloved associates. Just picture what the sand must have looked like after Paul boarded the ship and the crowd went back home. Footprints leading to and from the shore. Then nothing but knee prints—clustered together in the damp sand... a sight for God to behold. Long after the time and tide had washed away every print, the power of those prayers was still at work.[5]

I just love this young woman and her keen insight into God's Word. I wept as I read this, and wondered about the "knee prints" I'm leaving in the kingdom.

In early 1991, I spoke at a women's meeting in Mobile, Alabama. Prior to the meeting I had received a letter from a missionary to Brazil, Thelma Bagby. She wrote that she had read my book, *Empowered!*, (first edition), and that she would like to meet me. She told me that she knew we spoke the same language. Well, I knew I did not speak Portuguese. As I spoke the first night, Thelma, a small lady, stood in the audience and waved a handkerchief at me. After the service we met and walked together to a banquet that followed. I was not seated at her table, but wanted to be with her, so I got up, went to her table, and knelt at her side. I discovered then that the language she spoke was the language of the Holy Spirit. His presence was all over her face and in her words, and her joy confirmed it.

In a note she later sent, Thelma wrote, "Esther, you are a chosen vessel, with the particular, singular fragrance of Christ Jesus." I recorded her remarks in the front of my Bible. Little did I realize that her words to me from Paul's letter to the Corinthians would ten years later be the theme for my book, *A Garden Path to Mentoring* (New Hope Publishers).

Miss Thelma must have been praying that verse into my life. I did not realize until I'd finished writing the book that her words and prayers had so deeply touched my life. "In the Messiah, in Christ, God leads us from place to place in one perpetual victory parade. Through us, he brings knowledge of Christ. Everywhere we go, people breathe in the exquisite fragrance. Because of Christ, we

give off a sweet scent rising to God"
(2 Cor. 2:14 *The Message*).

A friendship had begun, and Miss Thelma
and I became pen pals. She introduced me to
John Baillie's little book, *A Diary of Private
Prayer*. Thelma shared with me that during
her first voyage to Brazil she noticed a young
couple that, at 5:30 each morning, made their
way to an upper deck of the ship and prayed
together. When she inquired about their
prayer time, they introduced her to Baillie's
book. She gave me a copy, and I've worn out
two others since!

Thelma was a woman known for her
prayer life. I asked her if I could send her my
travel calendar, requesting her prayers.

As I've recorded in, *Splash the Living Water*,
"not only did she pray for me, but when I got
back home from a speaking engagement she
would call me to accountability." She might
say, for example, "Where were you on March
25? I must know! What did God do? I was
not released from my knees on your behalf
until noon that morning."

As the chorus goes, "Surely the presence
of the Lord is in this place, I can feel His
mighty power and His grace." And, I would
add, surely the world is in need of more
prayers like those of Thelma Bagby. I was one
of many for whom she prayed, and only eternity will reveal all the Spirit was able to
accomplish through Thelma's prayers.

Some months after her death, I received a
call from Thelma's son, Dr. Dan Bagby.

I was surprised to hear his voice. He said,
"I'm home at mother's putting her things

away." My heart skipped a beat as I sensed our loss. "I know she loved you," he continued, "and prayed for you. I wanted you to know that I found your last calendar in her prayer chair. Esther, she prayed for you till the end."

It took me a moment to respond, "Thank you for this last blessing from your mother. I miss her so." Thelma borrowed the Spirit's activity, authority, and power through her prayers—so that it could become His power in and through others.

In the spring of 1999, I spoke to a group of women at First Baptist Church in Ruston, Louisiana. Women from sixty-one different churches came together for the Women's Refreshment and Renewal conference. For months the pastor's wife, Vicki Leavell, and I received prayer cards from the women. These cards shared Scriptures and promises that they were praying for the meeting.

The Spirit knew I needed those cards of encouragement. The week before I was to arrive, the mail brought a fat brown envelope addressed to me with a return address that read:

> *From Some Pray-ers*
> *206 Adam Circle*
> *Ruston, LA 71270*

I wept. As I told my husband, this could mean "From Some Prayers," or it could mean "From Some Pray-ers." This two-fold meaning did not go unnoticed. I was humbled, and I welcomed every one of their prayers. Those "pray-ers," using borrowed authority and

When we spend time every day in prayer and in His Word, the Holy Spirit empowers us to become persons filled and flooded with God Himself— able to touch our world for Christ. This happens as we spend quality time in His presence.

activity, made an impact on five hundred women for the glory of God. And that brown envelope is now mounted on the wall behind my computer, reminding me to this day that prayer is borrowed authority and activity.

Empowered by the Holy Spirit
to live a Spirit-directed life
to bow your heart toward God in prayer
to bend your life in surrender to God
to be obedient to the Spirit in your walk.

When we spend time every day in prayer and in His Word, the Holy Spirit empowers us to become persons filled and flooded with God Himself—able to touch our world for Christ. This happens as we spend quality time in His presence.

Doesn't that sound simple? It isn't, however. This is a discipline that, when it becomes part of your life, you will discover that you can't live without! You will feel a communion with the Spirit of God as you bend your heart in prayer before Him and ask Him to speak to you through His Word.

Some time ago I attended a Father's Day family reunion with my four brothers and two sisters. We experienced a wonderful weekend full of talking, laughing, crying, remembering, and praying. At the end of the weekend I went for a walk with my older sister, a beautiful, Spirit-filled woman. I said to her, "This has been so good, but what I really need is to get home and off by myself to think through some of the things we've said. I'm feeling a bit homesick for God right now." I had been caught up in four days of constantly being with family—we had not seen each other in such a long time. Yes, we opened God's Word and prayed each morning as a family, but that wasn't time alone with the Heavenly Father. I felt "homesick," a longing to be still before God.

The Quakers call this action "centering." Gordon MacDonald refers to it as "ordering your private world," and wrote a book about it by the same title. When we come before God in prayer and meditation, we "center" in that innermost place where the Holy Spirit speaks and works through us. We make room for the Spirit to work. To be empowered people of God, we must bend our hearts toward God in prayer and give the Holy Spirit control of everything.

Nell Bruce, a powerful prayer partner, sent me a tape. She had gone to visit Martha Franks, a longtime missionary to China, to learn about her days in China and the revival that took place there. Martha tells this story on the tape:

It all began with missionary Marie Munson. While Marie was serving in China, she heard that there was a great revival in Korea, and she wanted very much to go and see it. She felt that if she got to Korea she could bring back to her province of Hunan in China a "live coal" from the altar of revival in Korea.

One day, as Marie was praying that the Lord would provide her money to go to Korea to see that revival, the Holy Spirit spoke to her and

*To be empow-
ered people of
God, we must
bend our hearts
toward God in
prayer and give
the Holy Spirit
control of
everything.*

said, *"Marie, you don't need to go to Korea.
What I have done there, I will do here in
answer to prayer."* Marie said, *"Lord, if that is
what You wish, and if that is what it will take
to bring revival to China, I will do it."* She
prayed for twenty years before revival came to
her province.

One woman, using God's authority and
deity in prayer, touched the world. Oh, that a
"spiritual awakening" would come to the
United States! Many people believe that we
are not far from total "godlessness" in our
country. What a difference you and I could
make if we prayed on behalf of our nation and
our world that God's "Wind" would blow
fresh across our nation.

Are you willing to do this? Are you willing
to bow your heart before God for twenty
years, in the Spirit's borrowed authority, on
behalf of our nation?

Mrs. Martha Stroup lives in my community. Her late husband, Bill, served many years
ago as Director of Church Music for the
Florida Baptist Convention. After Bill's death,
Martha moved into the Baptist Tower building. Bob and I took her to lunch one day to
give her a copy of my new book and to share
fellowship with this wonderful woman of
God. She told us how lonely she gets for her
Bill, especially in the early morning when
they would read the Bible and pray together.

One morning as she was reading her Bible
and feeling sad, she got up and opened the
curtains. I wish you could have seen her eyes

as she described to us the beauty God had set in the sun rays as they hit the St. John's river. Her heart was so full. She began to sing, "How Great Thou Art." She went to the piano and began to play it and sing along. Now this is how she meets God every morning. She is, by the way, a wonderful pianist. Several mornings later, as she again played this great hymn, a knock came at the door.

It was the gentleman that cared for the building. As they greeted each other, he said, "Mrs. Martha, I've been outside your door each morning listening to your worship service. I know that song. May I come in and worship with you?" Her eyes sparkled as she told us this. "You don't suppose that was a bad thing to do at my age, do you?" she chuckled. "Well, it wasn't! We just went to the piano and had us a worship service singing to the Lord." How delighted God must have been as these two children praised Him and rejoiced in His greatness. Instead of thinking of prayer as our effort to persuade God to do our will, let's think of it as God burdening His people to do His will.

Peg Rankin writes in her book *Step into the Water*, "Prayer begins in the mind of God. God entrusts His burden to one or more Christians. The Christians, in turn, lift the burden as a petition. The petition then returns as an answer. The answer is acknowledged with praise to the Lord, who started the process in the first place. Who facilitates this downward-upward flow? God's Holy Spirit." [6]

I was privileged to participate in the worship service at a church in South Florida when Dr. Richard Wurmbrand spoke of his years of imprisonment in Rumania. I watched this lanky, tussle-haired gentleman as he made his way slowly to the pulpit and sat in a chair that faced the audience.

His Rumanian accent was hard to understand at first, but quickly the Spirit of God drew me in, and I tried not to miss a single word. He spoke of his fourteen years in prison for his faith and his activity as a pastor. My heart ached for my brothers and sisters that have paid the price of faith. I could not believe the stories of man's inhumanity to man. Eighty-two years this man has served God faithfully in ministry. His feet were crippled because the guards had beaten the prisoners' feet. His text was Isaiah 48:12–13. "Listen to Me, O Jacob. And Israel, My called. I am He. I am the First, I am also the Last. Indeed My hand has laid the foundation of the earth. And My right hand has stretched out the heaven; When I call them, they stand up together" (NKJV).

"I have been a prisoner of the faith," Pastor Wurmbrand said. "I learn in prison, like Paul, the cost of my faith. It cost me the loss of family, the death of friends, starvation, and cruelty beyond belief. But I learn, 'God is First and Last!' "

Some Christians in the prison wanted to have a communion service. They asked Pastor Wurmbrand how they could do this.

"We had nothing. So we clanged our chains together to the rhythm of 'This is the day . . . clank, clank. This is the day . . . clank, clank . . . that the Lord has made, . . .

clank, clank . . . that the Lord has made!' "
I'll never forget what he said next:
"Things can only be one kind. A car is a car.
You Americans . . . too much things. I learn
in prison . . . nothing can be anything! A
thing can only be a thing. Nothing can be
anything." I smiled sadly as he continued:
"If God of the universe created the world
out of nothing . . . we could have communion with nothing. We sent our message to
each other by Morse code. Together we broke
nothing . . . and remembered His broken
body . . . which cost Him everything. Then
we drank nothing . . . and remembered His
blood shed for us, His life, for ours.

"At first in prison. I could pray. I could
quote Scripture, and that carried me. As the
years went on, it grew more difficult to
remember. The four years in solitary confine-
ment, I got where I could not remember the
Lord's prayer. I wept in shame. The guards put
drugs in our food, that affected our memory,
but it was the only way to get food. We
slowly lost our memory."

At one time, all Pastor Wurmbrand could
remember was to sing "Jesus loves me." Then
he finally forgot that. He said the Lord's
Prayer until he forgot it. He then told God,
"Surely you know it by heart, you hear it so
much!" At the end, listening quietly to his
own heart beat, he prayed, over and over,
"Tick-tock Je-sus Je-sus (you know what I
mean, Father)."

He closed by proclaiming: "If the God of
Israel is the First and the Last, then I will trust
my heartbeat to God!"

As he made his way down to the front
row, the church stood to their feet to give him
a thunderous ovation. But I did not stand. I
sat and quietly wept for our brothers and
sisters who are imprisoned for their faith.

I want to learn, in all circumstances of my
life, to pray in the Spirit's authority, activity,
and deity—just one word: Je-sus!!

[1] Oswald Chambers, *My Utmost for His Highest*
(Westwood, New Jersey: Barbour and Company,
1963), 293.

[2] Ray C. Stedman, *Talking with My Father* (Grand
Rapids, Michigan: Discovery House Publishers, 1997),
113.

[3] Ibid., 115.

[4] Dr. R. Keith Parks, "What Is Jesus' Address?"
ch. 7, *Commission* 52 (August 1989), 79.

[5] Beth Moore, *To Live is Christ*,
(Nashville: Lifeway Press, 1997), 129.

[6] Peg Rankin, *Step Into the Water*, (Ventura, CA:
Renew Books, 1998), 92.

5

Fill Me

The Holy Spirit—Our Provision

Breathe on me. Breathe on me
Holy Spirit, breathe on me
Take Thou my heart, cleanse ev'ry part
Holy Spirit, breathe on me.

Edwin Hatch, "Holy Spirit, Breathe on Me" ©1937. Renewal 1965 Broadman Press. All rights reserved. Used by permission.

A city man, visiting a farm and noticing the water tank high in the air, asked the farmer how he knew when the water tank was full.

The farmer said, "You just stand here and turn on the pump." The water began to flow out and pour over the sides. "It's full," he said.

Jesus said "If anyone thirsts, let him come to Me and drink. He who believes in Me, as the Scripture has said, out of his heart will flow rivers of living water" (John 7:37, 38 NKJV). In 1 Thessalonians 3:12 we read, "May God our Father himself and our Master Jesus clear the road to you! And may the Master pour on the love so it fills your lives and splashes over on everyone around you, just as it does from us to you" (*The Message*).

Isn't this just like God, who pours out His Spirit to be our provision, and gives us all the power we need. What a promise!

The evidence of the presence of the Holy Spirit in our lives is the outflow. There must be a heart-hunger for the filling of the Holy Spirit. We must passionately and with faith desire the fullness of God in our lives. If there is a filling, there is also going to be a flowing. One who walks in the Spirit is pouring out that which the Spirit pours in—His joy . . . His peace . . . His patience . . . His goodness . . . His faithfulness—all that He desires us to be in Him. We are naturally drawn to persons who have these traits. We sometimes feel that if we can get close enough to that kind of person, these traits will spill over onto us.

And when it does, we are refreshed. But to maintain this refreshment we must stay before the Lord in His Word and in prayer. He is the only One who can do the filling. It does not come from another person—unless that Person is the Holy Spirit.

David wrote, "As the deer pants [longs for] the water brooks, so my soul pants for Thee, O God. My soul thirsts for God—for the living God; when shall I come and appear before God?" (Psalm 42:1–2 NASV). We must hunger for the fullness of God. Jesus said, "Blessed are those who hunger and thirst for righteousness, for they shall be satisfied" (Matt. 5:6 NASV). Do you thirst for a right relationship with Jesus above all else?

Paul prays for the Ephesians

that He would grant you, according to the riches of His glory, to be strengthened with power through His Spirit in the inner man; so that Christ may dwell in your hearts through faith; and that you, being rooted and grounded in love, may be able . . . to know the love of Christ which surpasses knowledge, that you may be filled up to all the fullness of God (Eph. 3:16–19 NASV).

What a promise. This is what I want, dear sisters in Christ. I want to know all the fullness of God.

Paul exhorts us: "Be filled with the Spirit," (Eph. 5:18 NIV). This is a process. It is an imperative command. It is also in the passive tense: God does the filling; we can't do it ourselves.

Acts 1:8 literally translates, "You shall receive the Holy Spirit coming upon you with power." The power that God gives you is not some thing . . . it is someone. It is the actual presence of Holy Spirit. This means anything God calls us to do, He has given Himself to help us do it. This is a wonderful promise. The Holy Spirit works in all believers to make them so like Christ that they will become an example to the world of what God is able to do with human beings. We are not here just to give a verbal witness. We are to become an actual sample of Christ.

The Holy Spirit equips us to bear fruit that will remain. Ephesians 5:18 translates, "be being filled." This statement is in the present tense, meaning "be filled continuously—day after day, month after month, year after year." When we use our automobiles, it takes gasoline to fuel the engine. When the car runs out of gas, there is nothing wrong with the car

When you and I do the work of the Father, we are using the power of the Holy Spirit. Like a car, we have to be filled continuously.

The filling of the Spirit is something that God does to me. In this process, I am enabled to do things I would not be able to do of my own strength.

except that it needs more fuel. When you and I do the work of the Father, we are using the power of the Holy Spirit. Like a car, we have to be filled continuously.

As I mentioned above, the verb used for "be being filled" is in the passive voice. The passive voice is used when the subject is acted upon.

The filling of the Spirit is something that God does to me. In this process, I am enabled to do things I would not be able to do of my own strength. It is no wonder, then, that Paul compares a Spirit-directed life to someone who has had too much wine. The person drinking is under the control of the wine. Likewise, as God fills our hearts and lives, we come under the influence of the Spirit.

No wonder the world marveled at the early church. It was under the power of the Holy Spirit. In a real sense, the church did not look like itself. Rather, it looked like Jesus and acted in the power of the Spirit.

Living a Spirit-filled life, we come to recognize the fingerprints of the Holy Spirit in our lives. Galatians 5:18 says, "But if we are led by the Spirit [indicating that the Spirit points the way], we are not under the law" (NKJV).

Perhaps we should ask ourselves how much of our lives do we allow the Spirit to fill? Consider that the idea of being filled with (by) the Spirit carries with it the idea of an agent—the one doing the filling. We must surrender our lives to the Spirit, become totally dependent on Him, and focus on being—not doing—for God. A life filled

with the Holy Spirit is the most powerful
sermon anyone can preach. It is a sermon that
leaves critics dumbfounded. A life like that
always points to Jesus, giving God the glory.

God's Provision for Us and Through Us

Bob and I stood with the congregation while
the missionaries marched into the auditorium
for the commissioning service. Our hearts were
full as Ray and Becky Brown marched to the
triumphant music. You see, we felt a part of
their journey—through prayer. From their first
trip as volunteers they had experienced the call
of God to go as full-time missionaries to a
people in North Africa! We know how to pray
for the Browns, as we keep in touch with them
through email. The following email came
Easter week of 1999:

Last night, on the way from the Missionary
Learning Center [MLC] in Richmond,
Virginia, to my Mom's house in Dallas, Texas,
the automobile struck a big pothole on I-20 in
Mississippi. Sensing trouble, I immediately
pulled over and found our right front tire flat
and the wheel rim bent. The new flashlight in
the car unfortunately had no batteries! As we
began to change the tire in the dark, another set
of headlights pulled quickly to the side of the
road behind us.

A woman got out of that car, walked toward
us, and asked if we could help her change her
tire as she had hit the same pothole! So I went
back and began to change her tire. As we

*talked, I found that she was a music minister's
wife at the Emmanuel Baptist Church in
Monroe, Louisiana. I was able to tell her all
about the African people to whom we were
assigned, that we had just been at MLC, training to be missionaries, and how the gifts of her
church through The Cooperative Program made
it possible for us to go to the mission field.*

*I finished putting on her spare and gave her
one of our prayer cards. She committed to taking
the prayer card back and challenging her church
to pray. Another church has joined our efforts to
reach this unreached group in North Africa!*

*Well, I walked back to our car and found that
we had inadvertently left the headlights on with
the engine off! It became immediately obvious
that the battery was dead! About this time, a
man pulled over to help us and we began to
hook up jumper cables. Another pair of headlights pulled over behind us.*

*Two women came asking if we could help
them change their tire—which was ruined by
the same "killer" pothole. I went back to
change their tire while Becky stayed with the
other man who was charging our battery. As we
talked, I found that these two women were
mother and daughter. It turns out that the
mother is the wife of the pastor of Ridgewood
Baptist Church in Graham, North Carolina.
The daughter is the wife of a youth minister at
a Baptist church in western Mississippi. I*

explained where we had come from and where
we were going, and told them about our heart's
cry for this African people. We handed them our
prayer card, and two more churches—in two
more states—have joined the prayer force for our
unreached people in North Africa!

Well, I went back to our car, and by this time
the car started. Oh, by the way, the man who
helped start the car heads the Department of
Public Health for the state of Mississippi. He
knew two doctors with whom I had trained in
my doctoral residency, and may one day be a
person who could come over and help us on a
volunteer trip to set up clinics where our North
African group lives. He also got a prayer card!

We have been praying for God to multiply
the prayer force for our unreached people in
North Africa! I have worried about how it will
happen, especially with our leaving the United
States so soon. God is so good to teach me that
He is the one who will cause His people to
pray. He is in control and He cares enough
about our people group that He would allow
three tires to go flat on a stretch of Mississippi
highway, that He might bring glory unto
Himself!

P.S. A wonderful couple from our church in
Jacksonville, Florida, met with us in
Birmingham, Alabama, the morning following
the flat and gave us a gift of money. It turned
out to be enough to buy the new wheel, which

God is so good
to teach me
that He is the
One Who will
cause His people
to pray.

Then I heard the Holy Spirit whisper to me, "I use older women, too." Every one of us is called to be obedient in a lost world.

is being put on the car right now—with $3 to spare. The tire was perfectly fine. God is so awesome!

Paul says it well: "My God shall supply all your needs according to His riches in glory in Christ Jesus" (Phil. 4:19 NASV).

Reggie McNeal, a pastor, author, and leadership development consultant, recently spoke on the present and future of the North American church. He is quoted in NETFAX, of Leadership Network:

[We are in] the second Reformation. The first Reformation returned the Word of God to His people. A second Reformation, now underway, is returning the work of God to His people as more and more believers come to understand and act on the belief that they are called, gifted, and empowered as ministers of the Gospel. The wrong question is "How can we employ more laity as church workers?"

This approach assumes that all viable ministry happens inside the church walls. The tough question is "How can we deploy God's priests to impact their world for Christ?" The challenge is to develop on-mission Christians who understand their primary ministry assignments to be where God has placed them: their homes, school, marketplaces, communities, and civic clubs.[1]

Mike Burczynski, pastor of Trinity Baptist Church, Moscow, Idaho, says that commitment is crucifixion.

"The Lord Jesus was ever calling for this 'death to self' extreme." In following Christ to a small church in a pioneer missions area, Mike left a thriving church in the South and took a 60 percent pay cut. That sounds like trusting God's provisions![2]

Jim Queen, former home missionary and now state missions director for the Illinois Baptist Convention, has ministered in the racially mixed, inner-city community of Chicago. He says: "Commitment is giving myself over to God completely to follow Him, to do whatever He says."[3]

Jim moved into the inner city, where pimps, drunks, and homosexuals live, because He believes that Jesus also came to save them. He is still empowering others to get outside the walls of the church.

According to former International Service Corps worker Mike Stroope, trusting God's provision is a "continual and radical redirection of life. [Its evidence is] values, lifestyle, and actions which result from constant examination and refocusing of life."[4]

A number of years ago I heard Mike's testimony. He said, "Pray for me and my family. My family will live in Europe, and I will go to work in a country where my family cannot live. I will be risking, but it would be more dangerous for me to be outside the call of God." As I heard Mike speak, I prayed, "Oh God, give us a thousand young men like Mike and his family, who are willing to risk their lives. Give us thousands of young men and women who are willing to risk in order to make a difference in the world." Then I heard the Holy Spirit whisper to me, "I use older women, too." Every one of us is called to be obedient in a lost world.

A church in Washington, D.C., sponsors a group that serves as a "lobby" for Jesus. They make a thorough study of the lives of the politicians who serve our nation. From newspapers, magazines, and interviews they try to discover what drives these political leaders, the principles by which they live, and how they vote. The group is interested in people in the powerful places in Washington as well as across our nation. The members will show up on the steps of the Capitol to meet a particular leader. When this leader comes from the building the group will tell him courteously, "We want to meet you and let you know that we wish to pray for you. We are interested in your work. We want to pray for you as you represent us in our nation's Capitol."

In one such encounter, a senator wept as he met the group. He was moved to know that he was not bearing his burdens alone—but had people who cared enough to pray for him personally.

Think what would happen if Christians prayed daily for our political leaders—global, national, and local!

The Spirit of God would be freed to do His work among those people in powerful places. Praying Christians can be God's provision for our government.

Darcy is a high school student who participated in a mission trip to Pennsylvania. The group planned to conduct a Bible club in one of the local communities. As they canvassed the neighborhood, looking for children to invite to the club, they met the mother of a mentally disabled child. The mother wanted her daughter to come to the club, too. The child was large and awkward. Darcy thought to herself, "I really wish this child would not participate."

But the next day the mother appeared at the club with her daughter. The other teenagers kept passing around the responsibility of looking after this girl. "You look after her." "No, you look after her!" Finally, the group turned to Darcy and said, "You need to look after her." The girls knew that Darcy has a younger brother who is mentally disabled.

"I didn't want to do it, either," Darcy recalls. But all week during the club meetings, Darcy befriended Nancy. They sat together, ate together, and did crafts together. "I really felt the Holy Spirit telling me that this is what I should be doing," recalls Darcy. "And when I became obedient to Him, it was a good experience for me."

"When the week was over, Nancy said to Darcy, "You're the best friend I have in the whole world, and you may be pretty on the outside, but you're prettier on the inside." Darcy had been the Spirit's provision of love for Nancy.

Jennie Robeson, a missionary nurse on a two-year assignment in Ethiopia, says she was overwhelmed by the needs in that country when she arrived.

She wasn't there very long before she began to question the value of her contribution to the ministry. She learned a valuable

*Now, why
would a man
from Asia,
who is a very
successful and
wealthy doctor
in the process
of moving to
Alabama,
stop at a car
dealership in
Alabama?
There is only
one reason.
Praise the Lord.
He is so good!*

lesson from a 1985 article in *the
COMMISSION* magazine.

In the article, Mary Saunders, a volunteer
to Ethiopia at that time, was quoted as saying,
"I've lived in African villages and seen pockets
of hunger, but not the vastness of the need
here. What I do here feels like a drop in the
bucket. But I remember the Swahili proverb,
'drop by drop, the bucket fills.'" [5]

God's provision through Mary and Jennie
may look like a drop in the bucket, but when
it's God's drops of love, it can fill an ocean.

The work of the Holy Spirit came
through the Internet recently. I read this with
fascination:

*This email story was written from a mother
to her daughter. There is a family living in
Alabama. Their little boy has a tumor in his
brain that is very rare and without treatment
will eventually kill him. But the only doctor in
the world that has experience in treating this
kind of tumor lives in Asia! The family, their
friends, and their church prayed for God's compassion even as the little boy grew sicker and
sicker. The family couldn't afford to take the
boy to Asia for the surgery. As a matter of fact,
they couldn't afford the surgery, even if the
doctor was in the US. They asked God to pre-
vent him from suffering, as he would eventually
die from the tumor.*

*The father of the boy is an auto salesman for
the local car dealership. One afternoon, a very
nicely dressed man stopped by the car lot. The*

dad met and talked to him. The customer said
that he didn't need a car. He certainly could
afford as many cars as he wanted, but he didn't
need one. Actually he wasn't really sure why he
had even stopped. The dad suggested they go
into his office and talk while they looked over
brochures. As they sat down, the dad introduced
himself to the customer. The customer's last
name was the very same last name as that of
the doctor in Asia who could operate on the
salesman's son!

The dad fell to his knees, praying and weeping. He couldn't believe that in his office was
someone with the very same last name as the
surgeon. Maybe he was a family member or the
doctor's brother. And, maybe, he might be able
to arrange for the doctor to help his son. The
rest of the staff of the car dealership began gathering around to see what was happening.

The customer was more than a little surprised
by the reaction he had gotten to his name. As
the father told the story about his son and his
illness, the customer began to understand. You
see, the customer was not a family member of
the doctor. He was the very doctor. He was in
the process of moving his medical practice from
Asia to a hospital in Alabama, which is only
two hours away from our little town.

He promised the father that as soon as he
completed his move to the US he would perform
the surgery on the little boy—free of charge.

I believe one reason the Christian community lacks joy today is that we are not telling about God's provisions in our lives and in His world.

Now, why would a man from Asia, who is a very successful and wealthy doctor in the process of moving to Alabama, stop at a car dealership in Alabama? There is only one reason. Praise the Lord. He is so good!

I recall a time when my parents were in a Canadian Bible school with no money, no food, and three small babies. My mother had just been informed by the landlord that the rent was about to go up. He had learned that another baby was on the way.

She set out for a walk, pushing the baby buggy and praying for food and another room to rent. In her despair over the situation, she became lost. A man and his wife, sitting on their front porch, heard her crying and offered to help. She told them the story and said she lived across the street from the Baptist church. When they learned that my father was a student at the Bible college, they immediately offered a room in their home, and for less rent. Then the man kindly showed her the way home. Upon arriving home, Mother discovered a box on her doorstep. It was full of groceries, with a note that read: "We felt God's Spirit directing us to help you. God Bless!" The note had no signature. Isn't that just like the Spirit—to provide and then not take credit for the provision?

Are you surprised? Our reaction to stories like these is often: "Can it be true?"

I wonder if Isaac believed it when Abraham said, "God Himself will provide a lamb." I wonder if Isaac believed the angel's voice. All I know is that Abraham named that place "The Lord will provide" (Gen. 22:9–14).

I wonder what the children thought as their parents complained for lack of meat and bread in the wilderness. All I know is that a Cloud appeared and a Voice from heaven said, "At twilight, you shall eat meat, and in the morning, you shall be filled with bread" (Exod. 16:12).

I wonder if the friends of Shadrach, Meshach, and Abednego believed that God would provide for them in the fiery furnace. All I know is that the king said, "Did we not cast three men bound in the midst of the fire? Look," he said, "I see four" (Dan. 3:24, 25).

When there seems to be no way, God will make a way. He does provide. Women filled with the Spirit live in the expectation of God's provision.

I believe one reason the Christian community lacks joy today is that we are not telling about God's provisions in our lives and in His world. How can we not tell? It will bless your heart to tell, and it will bless the family of God to hear. Besides that, someone who does not know God may overhear it and be drawn to Him.

In the Old Testament, God called His people to build an altar as a memorial of what He had done so they would not forget His faithfulness. Can we do less?

Remember Paul's words to the church in Corinth, "for they have refreshed my spirit" (1 Cor. 16:18 NIV). When you have been refreshed by the Spirit, you will be a refreshment to others.

God's Provision in
Our Needy World

We live in a diverse and dangerous world. Yet Jesus said, "My kingdom is not of this world" (John 18:36 KJV).

Let's look at some facts about our world:
- 7.1 billion people live on earth.
- 3+ billion of them are not Christian.
- 1.3 billion (26%) have never been given the opportunity to respond to the gospel.
- Society has lost its values. *Time* magazine called the 1980s the "Decade of Excess."
- 4 million women are beaten in their homes each year.
- The United States has one of the highest abortion rates among developed countries.
- Abortions in 1992 numbered 1,359,145.
- The highest abortion rate occurs among women between the ages of 18 and 19: 56 per 1,000 women.
- Every 26 seconds a teenager becomes pregnant.
- According to the SAMHSA (Substance Abuse and Mental Health Services Administration), a 1996 national household survey on drug abuse, 74 million (34.8%) of Americans ages 12 and older reported some use of an illicit drug at least once during their lifetime.
- One billion adults in the world are illiterate. The United States ranks

49th among 156 countries in literacy—a drop of 28 places since 1950.

- More "foreign" missionaries from other religions and cults come to the United States than to any other country in the world.[6]

When I read facts like these, I am overwhelmed. It will take Holy Spirit-filled Christians to reach a world in crisis. I need the Holy Spirit to remind me that it can be done, "drop by drop." We live in a culture that says "Me! Me! Me!" The culture preaches:

- Find out who you are.
- Do what feels good.
- Live and let live.
- Have it your way!

And yet researchers say that the Generation X is asking for guides. What an opportunity for the church! Jesus said, "If you love your life you will lose it. If you give it up in this world you will be given eternal life" (John 12:25 CEV). How radical. And what a risk: to die to self to make a difference in the world—claiming God's provision through the Holy Spirit.

Joe Wright, Pastor of the Central Christian Church, was asked to open the new session of the Kansas State Senate. Everyone was expecting the usual politically correct generalities. But what they heard instead was a stirring prayer, passionately calling our country to repentance and righteousness.

The response was immediate, with a
number of legislators walking out even during
the prayer. In six weeks, Central Christian
Church logged more than 5,000 phone calls,
with only 47 of those calls responding nega-
tively. Commentator Paul Harvey aired Pastor
Joe Wright's prayer on the radio and received
a larger response to this program than any
other program he has ever aired. In addition,
Central Christian Church is now receiving
international requests for copies of this prayer
from India, Africa, and Korea. The prayer is
reprinted below for your study and to place in
your heart:

"Heavenly Father, we come before You
today to ask Your forgiveness and seek Your
direction and guidance. We know Your Word
says, 'Woe on those who call evil good, but
that's exactly what we have done. We have
lost our Spiritual equilibrium and inverted our
values.

We confess that:

We have ridiculed the absolute truth of
Your Word and called it "pluralism."

We have worshiped other gods and
called it "multiculturalism."

We have endorsed perversion
and called it an "alternative lifestyle."

We have exploited the poor and
called it the "lottery."

We have neglected the needy and called it
"self-preservation."

We have rewarded laziness and called it
"welfare."

We have killed our unborn and called it "choice."

We have shot abortionists and called it "justifiable."

We have neglected to discipline our children and called it building "self-esteem."

We have abused power and called it "political savvy."

We have coveted our neighbors possessions and called it "ambition."

We have polluted the air with profanity and pornography and called it "freedom of expression."

We have ridiculed the time-honored values of our forefathers and called it "enlightenment."

Search us, O God, and know our hearts today.

Try us and see if there be some wicked way in us; cleanse us from every sin and set us free.

Guide and bless these men and women who have been sent here by the people of Kansas, and who have been ordained by You, to govern this great state.

Grant them Your wisdom to rule and may their decisions direct us to the center of Your will. I ask it in the name of Your Son, the Living Savior, Jesus Christ. Amen."

[1] NETFAX, No. 93, March 16, 1998, p. 1

[2] Deborah Price Brunt, "Commitment: Counting the Cost,"*Contempo*, 19 (July 1989), 7.

[3] Ibid.

[4] Ibid., 8.

[5] Robert O'Brien, "Viewing Africa: Ethiopia—Drop by Drop, Love Fills the Bucket," *The Commission* (September 1985), 58.

[6] •Statistics from the National Clearinghouse for the Defense of Battered Women (Web site).
•Statistics from National Drug Control Policy Information Clearinghouse (Web site).
•Literacy and Evangelism International (Web site).
•Campaign for Our Children (Web site).
•Focus on the Family (Web site).
•www.infoplease.com

6

Use Me

The Holy Spirit—Our Promise

Spirit of the Living God, fall fresh on me
Spirit of the Living God, fall fresh on me
Break me, melt me, mold me,
fill me, (use me)
Spirit of the Living God, fall fresh on me.

Daniel Iverson, "Spirit of the Living God"
© 1994 Birdwing. Used by permission.

Matthew 28:19–20 is often called "the great commission," but I fear we have made it "the great discussion." I also believe we should start the commission with verse 18: "And Jesus came up and spoke to them, saying, 'All authority has been given to Me in heaven and on earth. Go therefore and make disciples.'" How? The answer lies in His promise: "Lo I am with you always, even to the end of the age." This promise of power comes to us in the Person of the Holy Spirit, whom Jesus, in this authority, gives to each one of us. His dominion is everlasting. His Kingdom will not be destroyed. It is forever!

We have His promise!
We have His authority!
We have His presence!
We have His power!
What are we waiting for?

Luke 24:49 says, "And behold, I am sending forth the promise of My Father upon you; but you are to stay in the city until you are clothed with power from on high." John gives us the same promise in John 14:26: "But the helper, the Holy Spirit, whom the father will send in My name, He will teach you all things, and bring to your remembrance all that I said to you." Perhaps the key lies in that wonderful chapter on "abiding" (John 15). I am convinced that the secret to living in the promise of the Holy Spirit lies in our abiding faith. We abide in the vine, drawing all sustenance and nurture that the Father pours through us, and are clothed in the Holy Spirit. He tells us that apart from Him we can do nothing!

In my quiet time on April 2, 1999, I was using Prayer Patterns, part of *Missions Mosaic* magazine that lists the names of missionaries on their birthdays and where they serve. Cindy Dake, a marvelous writer, suggests reading Colossians 2:9–10 and praying these verses for the missionaries. I looked them up and before I could even read it, my eyes were diverted to the top of the page, where I had highlighted Colossians 1:29: "And for this purpose also I labor, striving according to His power, which mightily works within me." I had dated this verse on April 22, 1989 with the note, "*Empowered!* finished—Hilton Head Island, South Carolina." Bob and I had taken ten days off that year so I could finish writing the original version of *Empowered!*. On April 2, 1999, as I worked on the rewrite of this same book, the Father kindly showed me this

promise He had given ten years earlier as I
wrote the original manuscript. Tears began to
flow as I reflected on how kind the Father was
to show me this promise. It is still His power
that works mightily within me. God is so
much better to us than we deserve. His power
is mighty!

Oswald Chambers writes,

*You can never measure what God will do through
you if you are rightly related to Jesus Christ. Keep
your relationship right with Him, and whomever
you meet day by day, He is pouring rivers of living
water through you, and it is His mercy that He
does not let you know it. When once you are
rightly related to God by salvation and sanctifica-
tion, remember that wherever you are, you are put
there by God; and by the reaction of your life on
the circumstances around you, you will fulfill God's
purpose, as long as you keep in the light as God is
in the light.*

John 7:38 (NASV) says, "He who believes
in me, . . . 'from his innermost being shall
flow rivers of living water.' "

Strive to be a vessel for Jesus Christ
through which living water pours. Think of
the people who have been that refreshing
living water in your life. They may not have
even known that God was using them as a
river of joy in your life.

Now that you have His presence, consider
how you can be that river of life in the lives of
others.

*I am convinced
that the secret to
living in the
promise of the
Holy Spirit lies
in our abiding
faith. We abide
in the vine,
drawing all
sustenance and
nurture that the
Father pours
through us, and
are clothed in
the Holy Spirit.*

The Holy Spirit
Uses Willing Vessels

It seemed a mix-up that the lady that occasionally does my nails was not in, and I was given to Veronica.

As she began to work with me, we began the usual "chit chat." Then, all of a sudden, she began to open up about her sons, ages seventeen and nineteen.

I had shared with her that I was a Christian speaker and asked about her faith background. She said she had been raised in the church. Her husband died and left her a lot of money, but she wanted to work as a way to get out and meet people. Her sons were not happy with her because she had a boyfriend who was pushing her to buy a new home. She'd almost signed the papers, but he did not want to help with any of the finances! I asked her quite gingerly why he should help. She lowered her head in my presence and said she was living with him.

I try not to act surprised at today's living arrangements, but the Spirit whispered to me to ask about her sons. I asked, "How do your sons feel about this?" She lowered her head again, confessing that they were not happy. They said their father would be ashamed of her, and that the church would not like it either . . . . Hard answers to her question! They asked her to put the boyfriend out. She began to cry. As she caught her breath, I said, "Veronica, your sons are right. You can be proud of your sons. What you are doing is disobedient to what you know of God's Word, and it is dishonoring to your sons. What kind of an example is that for teenage boys?" I asked her if she was attending church.

"No," she replied. "But when I first came from Cuba I go to the one up here on the corner to learn to speak better English." She described the teacher, "Miss Linda," and I realized that she was talking about my church and my close friend, Linda Montgomery. I invited Veronica to our church.

She since has moved, and as far as I know she never came. But I shared in His authority and power, and I trust the results with the Father. I could not wait to tell my Monday morning prayer group about my encounter at the beauty shop, and to thank them for faithfully teaching English as a second language every Wednesday morning at the church—participating in the Holy Spirit's work.

Robert was raised in a "hollow" in the deep hills of Kentucky. His pastor helped him obtain a scholarship to attend Cumberland University, a Baptist college in rural Kentucky. Robert's roommate at Cumberland was David, a doctor's son. Over time, the two roommates learned about one another and the diverse backgrounds from which they had come.

One day David told Robert that he would like to see a hollow, so Robert took him to see Canada Town, a small community named for the Canada family. Mr. Canada, his wife, and seven children all lived in that hollow, and several of the children had married and built slab houses of their own there.

David was amazed at what he saw. These families were living in slab houses—one-room dwellings made from slab wood off trees, with no running water, indoor plumbing, or windows. Most of the adults had little or no education. Few could read or write. Most had many children. After seeing all this, David said, "We've got to do something to help these people!"

Robert and David started a program called Mountain Outreach. They enlisted college students to go with them into the hollows to help build better homes for the people. The homes were not elaborate—at that time they cost just three thousand dollars each.

Robert is now a pastor, serving as a missionary in Alaska. David is a medical missionary in Africa. But the Mountain Outreach program—building homes for folks in those Kentucky hollows—continues.

The Promise of the Holy Spirit Never Changes

In January 1998, I was awarded the Honorary Doctorate of Humane Letters by Cumberland University. This was a very special time as my family gathered to see me "hooded." After the degree was conferred, I made my way off the platform to greet friends and professors from the university. I noticed a young man patiently waiting in line to speak to me. As he approached I could see he had an early copy of *Empowered!* in his hands. He quietly introduced himself, saying, "My wife brought your book home and I read it. When I read the story of Cumberland College and the Mountain Outreach program, it touched my heart. I told my wife that I wished God would let me do something just like that for Him. In fact, we prayed that we could some-day work in such a program." He grinned. "I am now the director of the Mountain Outreach program, and I have come to thank you for writing this book. I'd be so honored if you would sign it for me and my wife." How precious of the Father to let me meet this young man and hear his story a whole year before I began this rewriting project! How mysterious are God's ways, and how wonder-ful is His Spirit to clothe us and minister through us—even when we know nothing about it. He is our provision! He wants us to be His obedient vessels.

The Holy Spirit is Faithful

Part of my job at the Home Mission Board (now the North American Mission Board) was to assign youth groups to mission trips. I sent many youth groups to that Kentucky hollow to assist the college students in build-ing those modest homes and to conduct Bible clubs. The teenagers worked alongside the college students—pouring cement founda-tions, putting up drywall, and performing other tasks involved in building a house.

After one such trip I asked a teenage girl about her experience. "What did you think?" I asked. "Are you different because of your Kentucky experience?"

"Oh Mrs. Burroughs," she began, "when I went there, I was worried about little things—like chipping my nail polish. After I was there a week, little things like that weren't impor-tant anymore. I've never seen such poverty.

Most of the adults had little or no education. Few could read or write. Most had many children. After seeing all this, David said, "We've got to do something to help these people!"

As we got up to leave and say our goodbyes, she reached out and touched my dress. "You are so beautiful," she said. She didn't mean me—she meant my lifestyle. Compared to her, I am rich.

It was so good for me to go there and to discover how much I have. Now I am even more grateful to the Lord."

One day after I had first learned of Mountain Outreach, I had the opportunity to visit Cumberland University. I was anxious to meet Robert Day.

I asked him if I could visit Canada Town to see the work the volunteers had done. "Are you positive, Mrs. Burroughs?" he asked. I told him I was very positive.

That afternoon Robert took me to visit two homes in the Canada Town hollow.

Our first visit was to the home of Linda. I'd never seen anything like it in my entire life. She invited us in, and when I sat down on the couch there was so little support, I almost went to the floor. My vision was in direct line of the kitchen table, which happened to be a large wooden spool—the kind upon which telephone wire is rolled. The walls were bare except for artwork the children had brought home from school.

Their beds—mattresses on the floor—were neatly made. The entire house was very clean and neat. Linda was very proud of it.

As we got up to leave and say our goodbyes, she reached out and touched my dress. "You are so beautiful," she said. She didn't mean me—she meant my lifestyle. Compared to her, I am rich.

Robert then took me down the hill to visit Mary, Linda's sister-in-law. I could hear Mary yelling and screaming at her children while we were still some distance from the door. There were seven of them—running all over the house

and over each other. When we entered the
house, Mary said to me rather loudly, "Sit
down!" I sat down on the sofa—this time I did
go all the way to the floor, my knees up to my
chin! It was an uncomfortable position, but
Robert wasn't uncomfortable. These were his
friends. We visited a bit, and then Mary said,
"Robert, I just can't get them math problems!"

Going over to her, Robert answered, "Mary,
I have trouble with them, too." He bent over to
help Mary with her third-grade-level math
homework. She was preparing for the GED
test. What a minister of grace. For a moment I
saw Jesus. Robert Day was the Holy Spirit's
provision to that community.

As we returned to the car, I could stand it
no longer. Tears flowing freely, I said, "Robert,
I had no idea there was that kind of poverty in
my nation! Thank you for what you have
shown me today, and for the Spirit of God I
sense in you.

I could not wait to get back to Atlanta to
tell my family about Canada Town. It changed
our Christmas celebration. Through my tears I
told them, "We can't afford to do Christmas in
this home like we did last year—not with the
hurt that is in the world, especially in Canada
Town." What a great time we had spending
Christmas money on presents for the people in
Canada Town. And it was a wonderful
Christmas for us in return.

The Promise of the Holy Spirit Enables His Church

Charles Roesel is pastor of First Baptist
Church, Leesburg, Florida. I talked with him

recently to get an update on their evangelism ministries. He said, "For thirteen years now, I have been leading the Leesburg church to live up to our slogan, 'The Church That Cares.'" As pastor, Roesel's vision to build "a church so spiritually equipped that any time someone sets foot on the property, regardless of the need—physical, emotional or spiritual—it will be met." He says that Matthew 25 serves as the biblical basis of what he calls "Ministry Evangelism." To that end, fourteen hundred-plus volunteer positions in eighty-two different ministries are "filled by God's people" from the Leesburg congregation. Just this month they have begun a Rapha Counseling center on campus, a medical clinic, and a legal counseling service. The church recently completed its "Ministry Village," which includes new buildings for its rescue mission for men and the women's shelter. Those two ministries date back to 1982 and 1989, respectively, and were previously operated in houses the church purchased across the street from its main facilities. Additional Ministry Village facilities include the Pregnancy Care Center, the Children's Rescue Shelter, and the Teen Home, as well as a furniture barn, clothing closet, and food pantry. Ministry Village is completely debt-free.

Recently they began a school of fine arts and a hospital ministry. The fine arts ministry teaches students everything from violin to creative movement.

"It reaches a cross-section of the city, since we have the only fine arts school in the area. We have many people bringing their children, which provides another opportunity for a gospel witness."

Roesel said the city hospital offered the church a registered nurse as well as malpractice insurance if the congregation would furnish a facility. "This may become the pilot project for ministry of this type across the nation— it's a 'win-win' situation!" Roesel smiles. "It saves the hospital a small fortune because we can provide care for ten cents on the dollar, and it gives us an opportunity to bear witness to everyone who comes. We're meeting medical needs of transients and those who can't afford hospital care."

This Leesburg church is truly being a church. The following story appeared in *SBC Life*, June/July 1998, p. 2:

When Charles Roesel moved to his new neighborhood almost two years ago, he didn't plan on using leaf removal as an evangelistic tool! But his approach to evangelizing through ministry led to such an opportunity.

Shortly after settling into his home, Roesel discovered that the neighbors who lived behind him had a skeptical view of organized religion, and were particularly resistant to the claims of Christianity.

During a casual conversation with his neighbor, Roesel noticed that leaves had collected on their roof, and asked why.

"Oh that's easy to explain," she responded in her British accent, "My husband is afraid of heights."

Soon afterwards, Roesel grabbed his leaf blower, ladder, and proceeded to remove the leaves from their roof.

"It was no big deal." he said.

Perhaps it wasn't to him, but the couple had

"It saves the hospital a small fortune because we can provide care for ten cents on the dollar, and it gives us an opportunity to bear witness to everyone who comes. We're meeting medical needs of transients and those who can't afford hospital care."

When we willingly surrender to the Spirit, we bow our hearts before the Father, we yield, and we surrender our lives—our all—to Him.

never experienced such an act of servanthood performed in the name of Jesus.

Within two weeks, they attended a worship service at FBC Leesburg. Over the next two weeks, they heard the truth of the Gospel several times. Within thirty days of the leaf removal, they both surrendered their lives to Jesus. Today they are both active in the ministries of the church.

"I could have spent two years debating the claims of Jesus. I could have given them Evidence that Demands a Verdict," *Roesel said. "But one loving act of servant evangelism did more that I could have ever done in that amount of time."* [1]

The Holy Spirit Shows Us Needs

In his book, *If You Will Ask*, Oswald Chambers writes,

The only one who prays in the Holy Spirit is the child, the child-spirit in us, the spirit of utter confidence in God. When we pray in the Holy Spirit, we bring to God the things that come quite naturally to our minds, and the Holy Spirit who . . . 'maketh intercession for the saints according to the will of God' (Romans 8:27) enables God to answer the prayer that He Himself prays in our bodily temples. 'That ye may be the children of your Father which is in heaven.' The Holy Spirit cannot delight in our wisdom; it is the wisdom of God He delights in. [2]

Have you ever seen a child, in utter dependence upon God, bow her head and ask

God for something? I believe this is what God
wants us to do—to have a childlike spirit as
we pray in the Spirit's authority. It is not
because we are helpless that we pray. We pray
because God is almighty. He is God. Dr. T.
W. Hunt has said, "The purpose of prayer is
twofold: first, to get to know God, and
second, to be a part of God's work through
praise and intercession."

When we willingly surrender to the Spirit,
we bow our hearts before the Father, we
yield, and we surrender our lives—our all—to
Him. When we surrender, we "give over" or
"give in" to a power within us that is greater
than anything we can do by ourselves. *The
Message* translates Matthew 5:13, 14: "Let me
tell you why you are here. You're here to be
salt-seasoning that brings out the God-flavors
of this earth. If you lose your saltiness, how
will people taste godliness? You've lost your
usefulness and will end up in the garbage…
You're here to be light, bringing out the God-
colors in the world. God is not a secret to be
kept. We're going public with this, as public as
a city on a hill."

I think one of the great barriers in the
evangelical church today is that we tend to
hide inside the walls of the church, or in what
I'll call "Holy." We make our friends there.
We pretty much all look alike, act alike, and
dress alike. We have lost our uniqueness, our
salt-seasoning. The salt flavor in us will draw
others to thirst for a living relationship with
Holy God. It is easy to form all our relationships with persons already inside the church.
We even have huge church complexes that

take care of the eating, schooling, recreation, education, and worship needs of the congregation—one does not have to go outside the church walls for much of anything. If we do not invite and bring the outsider in, then what is our reason for being? That would be like placing signs out front that say, "Members Only." What an affront to Holy God!

It is exciting to see the Holy Spirit at work. As I travel about this country, I meet men, women, and teenagers who are willing to be used in the power of the Holy Spirit. The Spirit of God works across denominational and local church lines all over the world today. The Holy Spirit can work anywhere He wishes. He is not the resource for a particular church, denomination, or religious group. Instead, the church is the resource for the Holy Spirit in the world. And who makes up the church? The people of God! My challenge to you, dear reader, is to be a person of God through whom the Holy Spirit can work.

Several years ago Bob and I wrote a musical. In one of the songs, I paraphrase Matthew 25. The song is entitled "When, Lord:"

The King is coming in all His glory,
To gather the people of every nation around Him.
Some will sit at His right hand; some will sit at His left.
To those on His right, He will say:
"Come on in, you're welcome.
Come on in and share My kingdom.
Come on in and spend eternity with Me eternally,
For I was hungry, and you fed Me;
I was thirsty, and you gave Me drink.
I was naked and you gave Me your clothes.

I was sick and you took care of My needs.
I was in prison and you paid My bail.
Come on in, you're welcome!"
"When, Lord, when did we do these things for You?"
"When you fed the hungry, that was Me.
When you helped the hurting, that was Me.
When you clothed each other in My care, that was Me.
You do it all for Me!"

To those on His left, He will say:
"Depart, now! My kingdom is not yours.
Walk away, now. You did not see the least of these;
So why should you see Me?"

"Why, Lord, are we not welcome?
Why, Lord, is Your kingdom not for us?"
"You chose not to feed Me, as you ignored the hungry.
You chose not to visit Me, as you neglected strangers.
You chose not to clothe Me, as you wrapped up warm yourself.
You chose not to heal Me, as you overlooked my pain.
You chose not to love Me, as you loved those already loved.

Does this text describe any local church congregations today? Are we so busy looking after ourselves that we do not see the hungry, the imprisoned, the hurting? Have we insulated ourselves inside the walls of our own fortresses? The Holy Spirit is ready to release His power in us to minister to the hungry, the illiterate, the disenfranchised, the refugees, the strangers. Child of God, this is exactly what it means to live in the power of the Holy Spirit.

Jesus said to His disciples, "Come, follow me." He did not say, "Decide for me." He asked them to yield to His authority in their lives. He asked them to give up everything. "Don't take

The Holy Spirit is ready to release His power in us to minister to the hungry, the illiterate, the disenfranchised, the refugees, the strangers.

anything with you. Don't take a second coat.
Don't take a money bag. I'll walk before you
and provide your needs," He told them.

I sometimes think that this must have been
simple for those disciples—fishermen, tax col-
lectors, doctors, and other laymen whom He
called. After all, Jesus Himself called them. But
then the truth dawns on me that Jesus Himself
has called me also. I have to remember this
when, every Friday, as I head out the door,
get into my car, and drive thirty-six miles to
the airport to catch a flight to a city where I
will speak to a group of women.

I would not go, except that He has called
and empowered me to do so. I cry to Him to
fill me and minister through me as I travel and
speak to these women.

When we are empty, the Holy Spirit calls
us to come to Him in prayer and assures us of
His presence as He fills us up. Henry Blackaby,
author of *Experiencing God*, says, "In prayer
before God, what happens is we adjust our
lives so that we will come into harmony with
all the resources and activity of God. If I go
into my work place to figure out what I am
going to do or what my church is going to do,
and I haven't taken time to pull my life into
harmony with what God is already doing out
there, then how can I join God in what He is
already about? Through prayer God brings our
lives into harmony with Who He is and what
He is about, and then He asks us to follow."

The Holy Spirit
Uses Us to Meet Needs

I know of a church in the West that began a

special ministry to senior citizens, with senior citizen Bible clubs and other activities. Ion, who was eighty-nine years old, had no relatives to visit her in the nursing home. Women and men from this church began to visit Ion and discovered that she could play the piano. She had played piano in a bar, and could play all kinds of music. The group became involved with Ion on a regular basis. They brought her food and remembered her birthday. At ninety-one years of age Ion came to the Bible study and asked Jesus Christ to come into her life. At ninety-two she was baptized, and at ninety-three she went to be with her Heavenly Father. Ion had been one of the "throwaways" of our nation—until someone clothed in the Holy Spirit came to minister to her.

Eunice Perryman Milligan left her job at sixty to volunteer with an International Mission Agency. She traveled all over Africa and much of the US, using her business skills and entertainment gifts to minister to missionaries. When she returned home, she wrote a book about her journey, titled *Simply His*. We can trust the Spirit to use us and give us opportunity to share with others for the glory of God. The reason I know so much about Eunice is that two years ago she married my widowed, ninety-one-year-old father, David. They still serve God in Pell City, Alabama. What about you, my friend? Where does Jesus want to take you today? How does He call you to join Him in Kingdom work?

Mae is a retiree who joined God at work. Mae took early retirement as a high school

We can trust the Spirit to use us and give us opportunity to share with others for the glory of God.

business teacher. At age fifty-five she volunteered for a two-year stint in the Peace Corps.
After that she became a regular volunteer
through a denominational mission agency. At
least four to six months out of every year,
Mae lives somewhere overseas, fulfilling short-
term volunteer assignments in the power of
the Holy Spirit—changing lives and being
changed.

I emailed my friend Trudy Johnson, project coordinator for Christian Women's Job
Corps, to ask about volunteer projects that are
making a difference, and to hear stories of
how God's Spirit is moving through people in
everyday situations. She sent me an email
she'd received from a woman named Shirley:

From: Shirley
Sent: Wednesday, April 14, 1999
11:10 A.M.
Subject: Answered prayer
Jan 27th, I sent an email to all of you requesting
prayer for the current class of CWJC (Christian
Women's Job Corp). We were amazed at what God did
through your contribution of prayer for this class.
Remember, I told you it was as if there was a visible
oppression in the room—dissension, critical attitudes, etc.
It was on a Wednesday that I sent the request. By
Friday, our director Sarah Weaver said there was a
change of spirit, and that some of the women went to
"Heaven's Gates, Hells Fire," a drama presented by
Bacon Heights Church. seven were saved! One woman
invited her husband, and he, too accepted Christ! The
session was great, and graduation was awesome! You
were a part of that victory. You participated in the salva-
tion choice of each one of those individuals.

You are just as much a part of our CWJC as if you were physically in the sessions, and we want to tell you how much we appreciate you and your efforts to be faithful to what God called you to do that week as you prayed for those women. That class of women have 42 children in their homes, and in a few years, those children will head 42 families and have for themselves 120 or so children, and so it will continue to multiply.

Your prayers will continue to bear fruit as long as there is a lineage of any one of those women alive! WOW! Now it is easy to see the power of prayer and its effect on CWJC and the lives of so very many. Pray for this program. Lift up to our Father each program, and ask Him to put a hedge around the classrooms so Satan cannot prohibit the working of the Holy Spirit in those lives. Truly, America will be impacted for better or for worse from the nucleolus we call Christian Women's Job Corps. Talk about it to others and put it on every prayer list of which you are aware. Blessings on your coming out and your going in, this day.

Shirley!

Pray for families, the church, the nation, the world. Prayer is work—yes: it is His work. We join Holy God in bringing about His kingdom when we pray. What higher calling can there be? What loftier goal?

One of the passions of my heart today is to raise up another generation of women who pray. Pray for families, the church, the nation, the world. Prayer is work—yes: it is His work. We join Holy God in bringing about His kingdom when we pray. What higher calling can there be? What loftier goal?

Our purpose in prayer is to join God in His work. Perhaps the reason we don't take the time to pray is that we don't always see the results. The results, remember, are the work of the Holy Spirit. We pray because He asks us to pray—using His name, His authority, His deity.

Another passion of mine is to raise up
a generation of women who claim God's
promises as found in His Word—underlining
them, praying over them, dating them when
God answers, and teaching other women to
trust God's Word. And going one step further:
to tell each other about it in praise and celebration. This encourages the body of Christ
and lifts up the name of Jesus. What an awesome thought: that your prayers can affect
generations to come. Pray, women. Pray!

To be Empowered by the Holy Spirit—
to live a Spirit-directed life:
Bow your heart toward God in prayer.
Bend your life in surrender to God.
Be obedient to the Spirit in your walk.

For some time, I have felt led to give to
The *Jesus* Film Project. I love getting the
Campus Crusade newsletter that tells about
the victories and the needs related to this
Project. Certainly it has been directed by the
Holy Spirit. Millions are hearing and seeing
the Jesus story in their own language for the
first time. The latest newsletter includes the
following story:

*The story begins fifteen years ago in Indonesia—one
of the largest Muslim countries on earth. For a little 18-
month-old girl named Novi, life had already brought a
harshness far too great for such innocence. Her father was
a fisherman, but weeks without a catch had brought
hunger into their household.*

*One night, frustrated and drunk, he hurled a burning
oil lamp at Novi and her mother! The shattered glass
and burning oil flew into Novi's eyes. Except for a small
corner of her left eye, she was left blind. She would never*

see again. *Or so she thought ... until August of last
year. It was then, fifteen years after Novi's devastating
experience, that her aunt came to her and offered a special
invitation. She had heard about a group of men coming
to show the "JESUS" film in their own language. Before
they left to see the "JESUS" film ... they prayed for a
miracle—that Novi's sight would be restored ... As they
sat and listened to the film in the darkness of the night,
she heard words that could have been her own: "Jesus,
Son of David, have mercy on me!" It was the blind
beggar crying out to Christ, asking Him to heal him.
Novi's aunt silently cried out to God in prayer, trusting
for a miracle.*

*Then it happened! Novi felt something brush her neck.
"What was that?" she exclaimed. "It is Jesus," her aunt
replied. And then she felt it again ... but this time it
was on her eyes—like fingers brushing against her eye-
lids. Little did Novi know that the film on the screen
was showing the same thing ... Jesus touching the
beggar's eyes ... When the "fingers" left her eyes, Novi
opened them and discovered that, when she looked up at
the screen, she could see Jesus. Novi was healed!*

*... Having known of Novi and her blindness for
years, everyone at the showing was awestruck and thrilled
... the same wonder spread to other villages as Novi and
her aunt traveled...sharing the incredible miracle.*

*When the Muslim villagers saw Novi, whom they had
known when she was blind, their hearts were touched by
the message of her Healer ... As a result, hundreds of
people have come to Christ, and the area churches are
still growing!*[3]

A team of people using their gift, producing the film in every language group possible,
racing against time: these people are being
used by God's Spirit to share the gospel.

When you pray, "Father use me," He will.

Hundreds of people give money and time to make this film possible, a little girl is healed, and God gets the glory forever.

When you pray, "Father use me," He will.

You're concerned about the hungry in the world, millions who are starving … and you ask, "What can I do?"

feed one

You grieve for all the unborn children murdered every day … and you ask: "What can I do?"

save one

You are haunted by the homeless poor who wander city streets … and you ask: "What can I do?"

shelter one

You feel compassion for those who suffer pain, sorrow and despair … and you ask: "What can I do?"

comfort one

Your heart goes out to the lonely, the abused and the imprisoned … and you ask: "What can I do?"

love one

Remember this, my child … two thousand years ago the world was filled with those in need, just as it is today, and when the helpless and the hopeless called to Me for mercy, I sent a Savior …

Hope began with only one!
—B. J. Hoff[3]

Dr. John Sullivan, Executive Director of Florida Baptist Convention, heard S. M. Lockridge preach the following about the power of Jesus Christ:

*If you decided to destroy the power of Jesus Christ,
what would you use for power to destroy His power?*

*You could not destroy the power of Jesus Christ or the
Holy Spirit by fire, because He would refuse to burn.*

*If you decided to destroy His power with water, He
would walk on it.*

*If you tried to destroy His power with a mighty wind,
He would stand up on a boat and say, "Peace be still,"
and it would lie down at His feet and lick His hand.*

*If you tried to use death, He'd clean out the grave and
make it a decent place to wait for the resurrection.*

What would you use for power to destroy His power?

Listen, Christian, You are clothed in that
power and that power is clothed in you.
Claim it! Jesus said, "All power is given unto
me in heaven and in earth" (Matt. 28:18
KJV). All the power of God was invested in
Jesus Christ, and all the power of Jesus Christ
is invested in the church—which is you and
me. We are the body of Christ in this world—
the scattered body of Christ. When we bow
our hearts before the Father in prayer, surrendering ourselves in obedience, we will be
empowered by Him to be witnesses of what
Jesus Christ has done in our lives. Claiming
the power of the Holy Spirit you are:

Empowered by the person
of the Holy Spirit
Empowered by the purifying work
of the Holy Spirit
Empowered by the power
of the Holy Spirit

If we claim this power, God's Spirit will begin to control our lives. When this happens... My prayer is: God, clothe me in your Holy Spirit, and make me willing to bow my heart, to bend my knee, and to be obedient.

Empowered by the presence
of the Holy Spirit
Empowered by the promise
of the Holy Spirit
Empowered by the provision
of the Holy Spirit

If we claim this power, God's Spirit will begin to control our lives. When this happens...my prayer is: God, clothe me in your Holy Spirit, and make me willing to bow my heart, to bend my knee, and to be obedient.

[1] Michael Chute, "Ministry Evangelism: Touching Lives, Changing Hearts, "*SBC Life*, June/July 1988, 1-3.

[2] Oswald Chambers, *If You Will Ask* (Grand Rapids: Discovery House, 1965), 57.

[3] The Jesus Film Project Newsletter, A Ministry of Campus Crusade for Christ International, March 1999.

[4] B. J. Hoff, © 1985, Abbey Press, St. Meinrad, Indiana reprinted with permission.
All rights reserved.